When Two or Three Are Gathered

Spiritual Stories by Contemporary Episcopalians

Edited by

Danielle Elizabeth Tumminio
and Kate Malin

Cover art by Caroline Coolidge Brown
Interior design by Carole Miller
© 2013 by Forward Movement
All rights reserved.
ISBN 978-0-88028-364-9
Printed in USA

Library of Congress Cataloging-in-Publication Data

When two or three are gathered : spiritual stories by contemporary
Episcopalians / edited by Danielle Elizabeth Tumminio and Kate
Malin. --
1st ed.
     pages cm
  Includes bibliographical references.
  ISBN 978-0-88028-364-9
  1. Episcopalians--Religious life. 2. Spiritual life--Episcopal
Church.
  3. Christian life--Episcopal authors. I. Tumminio, Danielle
Elizabeth.
  II. Malin, Kate.
  BX5933.W44 2013
  283.092'2--dc23

                                   2013023801

 Forward Movement
412 Sycamore Street
Cincinnati, Ohio 45202
www.forwardmovement.org

Scripture quotations are from New Revised Standard Version Bible,
copyright © 1989 by The National Council of the Churches of Christ in
the United States of America. Used by permission. All rights reserved.

When Two or Three Are Gathered

Spiritual Stories by Contemporary Episcopalians

Edited by

Danielle Elizabeth Tumminio
and Kate Malin

Forward Movement
Cincinnati, Ohio

TABLE OF CONTENTS

Introduction

Every person has a story, an evolving narrative of events and relationships, physical and emotional sparks. In this volume, we present stories by our contemporary community of saints that tell how their faith strengthened, challenged, and grew within them.

We are excited about this project because these stories paint a picture of what it means to be an Episcopalian today. Episcopalians are united by worship, which tells the story of our faith through our common prayer. Yet Episcopalians are like fingerprints, and no two perceptions of our faith are the same.

By asking Episcopalians to tell their spiritual stories and collecting them in this anthology, we hoped what might emerge was not only our tradition's diversity but also its unity. That's why we asked twenty-two participants to describe a moment where they experienced God's presence. This is what we define as a spiritual story.

We suggested they consider the activity a spiritual microautobiography; rather than squeezing their life story in three pages or less, we requested they focus on a single event, memory, or image from their spiritual life that was important in some way. We also asked that they frame their story using a passage from *The Book of Common Prayer*, because it is a book unique to, and cherished by, members of our denomination.

We did our best to seek out a variety of voices. Our participants include members of the laity as well as bishops, priests, and deacons, and they range in age from eleven up through the retirement years.

We made a conscious decision to edit the stories as minimally as possible in order to preserve the voice and theology of the participant, even when it differed from our own. We also respected the participants' ways of writing and thinking about God. For some, it was theologically important to use gender-specific pronouns as well as capitalization (i.e., He or Him), and for others, it was not. We decided personal theology should trump capitalization consistency. One editorial choice we did impose upon the stories was to cluster them together using the Baptismal Covenant promises, which are taken from *The Book of Common Prayer*, pp. 304-305.

At the end of every section, readers will find workshop material themed by each promise. Each workshop may be held in one or two sessions. In a single-session workshop, participants will talk over the discussion questions and then write a spiritual story on their own time using the prompts. If the workshop is split into two, the first session will be based upon the discussion questions; then participants will go home and write a spiritual story based upon the prompts. In the second session, one or more workshop members will share their story, with others providing theological and literary reflection. If the workshop is split into two, the opening and closing prayers may remain the same for each. We envision that each section's workshop could stand alone, or they could be used together as a Christian formation series.

Though many of the stories in this collection demonstrate an outward focus that illustrates how Episcopalians live their faith in the world, we know that writing and telling one's spiritual story has an inward focus too. So in the workshops, we were mindful to include questions that lead individuals to think about how their own transformation uplifts them to transform the lives of others.

Because after all, transforming lives is what being Episcopalian is all about. As the theologian Frederick Denison Maurice wrote in *The Kingdom of Christ*, "Human relationships are not artificial types of something divine, but are actually the means, *and the only means*, through which man ascends to any knowledge of the divine." It is our hope these stories reflect the myriad ways that our experiences help us understand God's desires for us. And we hope that through this understanding, we will form a stronger Episcopal community, equipped to be God's hands in the world.

— The Rev. Danielle Elizabeth Tumminio
— the Rev. Kate Malin

Acknowledgments

WE ARE THANKFUL to Caroline Coolidge Brown for graciously allowing us to use her painting *Lamb of God* for the cover of this book. She shares her spiritual story and the inspiration for the painting in the fourth section of the book.

We thank members of the Church of Our Redeemer in Lexington, Massachusetts, for testing out the workshops included in this volume.

We invite you to share your stories on our website: **spiritualstories.forwardmovement.org**.

Praying

Celebrant

> *Will you continue*
> *in the apostles' teaching*
> *and fellowship,*
> *in the breaking of bread,*
> *and in the prayers?*

People

> *I will, with God's help.*

Eva Suarez

On the Other Side of Loneliness

And now, as our Savior Christ has taught us,
we are bold to say...

—*The Book of Common Prayer*, p. 363

As an Episcopalian, sometimes I can forget to keep it simple. Our liturgy is so complex and rich, maintaining a sense of tradition even as we write new hymns and new prayers and daily challenge our ideas of what it means to be Christ's body in the world. That vigor is important, but without reflection, it can get away from me. And it's not only in church, but in life as well. Our modern world has made it possible to have a screen in front of me every minute of every day, to always be reachable, to always have something to do. Sometimes

I need a strong reminder to put those pressures aside. I need a reminder that I feel God's presence most when I strip away pretense, when I force myself to let go of my safeguards and invite God into my doubt and fear the same way I do my joy and praise.

One evening last summer, I found myself overwhelmed and seemingly alone. At twenty-one, I was in the midst of the discernment process for the priesthood and preparing for my senior year in college. I was working full time at a community center attached to a church, and living on my own for the first time, out in Brooklyn. It was exciting and challenging, and I felt constantly pushed—what was this new future I was imagining for myself, and for the church? What possibilities were out there? What was my life going to look like in a year? Could I even handle it? I was afraid to be afraid. I answered my questions with new questions and kept looking for new books, new people, new experiences. But that's not how doubt works, even when you're idealistic and twenty-one, and it caught up with me.

After a draining day at work, I felt depleted and nervous. A trip to the bank after work was sobering, and I worried how I would eat for the next week. The usually exciting subway ride felt overwhelming, the crush of people around me too much to bear. I let myself into my apartment and noticed sadly that my roommates weren't home—I didn't know them well, but I was hoping for something, anything to distract me. In the half-light, I sat on the edge of my borrowed bed, facing a bay window. This new view had been thrilling a month ago, but now it just felt lonely. Even scarier was the thought that in a few months this too would be gone, and I had no idea what would take its place. It wasn't the novelty that scared me, but what it stood for. I was firmly out of my teens, and the life that had felt so stifling in high school was actually the easiest it was ever going to get—the rest was up to me, and I didn't know if I could handle the challenge.

Struggling to center myself, I wanted to pray. Pressing the heels of my hands against my eyes, I lay down on my bed, trying to calm my racing thoughts. I tried to clear my mind, to get myself into the prayerful space I thought I knew so well, but it only made me feel more alone. I didn't know what to say to God to bring Him close to me, to make Him understand. This process of discernment, deciding to give my life to God—wasn't that supposed to make this easier? I felt unmoored. Words stumbled out of my subconscious, and I spoke them aloud, letting them fill the empty room. I said the Lord's Prayer.

At first, I let the words just be sounds, letting the rhythms calm my breathing, savoring their measure. I repeated the prayer again, and again, meditating on the words. It's the first prayer I ever learned, scrawled on construction paper in first-grade Sunday School, adorned with glitter glue. I had accepted the words so simply then, learned by rote, and it had been a long time, longer than I wanted to admit, since I had let them surprise me. The words were at once so simple and so powerful, so full of trust. "Thy kingdom come, thy will be done"...that is not a question or even a request for something I could simply grasp. Wherever the kingdom, whatever your will, let it be, Lord.

And to forgive me my trespasses, and those of others? To lead me from temptation and evil? There is no hiding there, only the recognition that sometimes I fall short, both in my own life and in my estimations of others. To ask that question doesn't give away any secrets but requires trust in grace, a trust that I freely give others but so often forget to receive. It is a chance to learn forgiveness, for myself and others.

The sensation of relief built slowly as I prayed, washing over me. I felt the presence of my Father, who art in heaven, as I prayed the way His Son had taught. My worries seemed not only small but distracting—walls I had put up between myself and the Holy Spirit, putting my concerns about success and appearances and comfort first, as if the life I wanted to live would be on my terms, not God's.

I wish I could say that since that moment with God my spiritual life has been perfect, that I've never felt doubt or fear; I've never done anything wrong. But I'm a human being. I can say, however, that the Lord's

Prayer has been rendered brilliantly new, lighting my soul up every Sunday. Its sheer simplicity and pure faith make it a challenge and a joy. I'm not reaffirming God's promise to me, or His presence in my life—because He does that, everyday. I am reaffirming that I hear His call and I feel His grace, and that I'm ready to hold up my end of the bargain. There is a reason we are bold to say these words.

———————■———————

Eva Suarez graduated from Columbia University and is persuing ordination in the Diocese of Washington. She is currently undertaking a dual degree program in divinity and social work at Union Theological Seminary and CUNY Hunter. In addition to her studies, she works at Charlotte's Place, the community center that is a part of Trinity Wall Street.

When Two or Three Are Gathered

Deathbed Reality

Depart, O Christian soul, out of this world;
In the Name of God the Father Almighty who created you;
In the Name of Jesus Christ who redeemed you;
In the Name of the Holy Spirit who sanctifies you.
May your rest be this day in peace,
and your dwelling place in the Paradise of God.

— THE BOOK OF COMMON PRAYER, P. 464

WITH THESE WORDS, we anointed the body of Pat, one of my closest friends. Her daughter and I kept vigil as the corpse cooled and stiffened and turned a darker shade of brown.

Pat was a deeply spiritual person who had explored many pathways and discovered many secrets of prayer. An associate of the Order of the Holy Cross, she was mother-confessor and advisor to many of the monks.

She took the Benedictine ideal of hospitality seriously. Her house was always open to guests, her table groaning with remarkable gourmet fare. Vestments, exquisite and simple, flowed from her sewing machine. Musically accomplished, Pat and her husband Don stabilized our small parish choir. Mathematically precise, she could balance parish books to the penny.

All her life, Pat's body had been something less than a friend to her. But age forty-nine proved apocalyptic, when back surgery precipitated a massive heart attack, requiring a multiple bypass operation. At first, necessity mothered invention: snail's pace recovery turned Pat from Martha into Mary as she shifted from driving all over the Los Angeles basin for meetings to embracing a contemplative vocation of offering others to God in prayer. But people are starved for God and flock to any who signal knowledge of how to take steps in God's direction, so year by year, her list of spiritual directees swelled. She was in demand for quiet days and became a leader on the board of our diocesan center for spirituality. Bite by bite, her low-fat diet was forgotten; appointment by appointment, her naptime was ignored, until suddenly she was slammed into the hospital for a second bypass surgery.

Because—like me—Pat was a daily Eucharist person, I took the sacraments to her regularly: oil for healing, Body and Blood of Christ for eternal life. From her hospital bed, she played the peacemaker, using feeble strength to reconcile estranged friends.

One rushed day after her second hospital release, I went by between errands to celebrate a Eucharist at Pat's home. Running on automatic pilot, I used the Sunday propers, Luke's Gospel for the Feast of Christ the King: "Jesus, remember me, when you come into your kingdom...Truly I tell you, today you will be with me in Paradise" (Luke 23:42-43).

I reproached myself as I drove away: why hadn't I remembered the oil and used the special readings for healing services? The answer came three hours later. Pat's daughter phoned from the hospital with the report: sudden irregular heartbeat, dash to emergency room, frantic heart massage, death in twenty minutes. Gospel promise turned prophetic: "Today, you will be with me in Paradise!"

Usually, death hurts the survivors, ripping up deeply rooted connections, leaving muscles and sinews dangling. My relationship with Pat had been a good one. This time, the pain was sharp and clean, not knotted by guilt or tangled with regrets. The remarkable thing was that for me, her death rent top-to-bottom the veil between this world and the wider reality of God's love. Beginning with that death-bed anointing, and for about a month afterwards, I lived with a vivid awareness that—as wonderful as this solid, chunky, colorful world is—it is an ephemeral shadow-copy of that wider reality of Divine Love which is far stronger than death. I kept on experiencing the overpowering reality of God, outclassing everything, but vice-gripping us—Pat and me, all of humankind—binding us in unbreakable community. "Into your hands...we commend"...our sisters and brothers, our very own selves—into your hands, where we are, always have been, and will be forever!

Marilyn McCord Adams is an Episcopal priest and a sometime professor of philosophy and theology. For twenty-one years, she taught medieval philosophy and philosophy of religion at UCLA, before moving to Yale Divinity School and the Religious Studies Department where she taught historical and philosophical theology. She then moved to Oxford University, where she was Regius Professor of Divinity and Canon at Christ Church Cathedral. She has published a number of acclaimed books and articles on medieval theology and the relationship between God and evil. Besides these academic works, she has also published a book of sermons entitled *Wrestling for Blessing* (Church Publishing, Inc., 2005) and a book of prayers titled *Opening to God: Childlike Prayers for Adults* (Westminster John Knox Press, 2008).

Breaking Together

The Celebrant breaks the consecrated Bread.

A period of silence is kept.

Then may be sung or said

> *Alleluia. Christ our Passover is sacrificed for us...*
>
> — THE BOOK OF COMMON PRAYER, P. 364

IT HAPPENED ON A FRIGID, dove-grey winter morning, as students gathered before classes in the cozy seminary chapel for Eucharist. The priest serving that morning had recently fallen and shattered her wrist, which was now enshrouded in cast and sling. Unable to lift her arm to break the bread, she asked if I would help. As the phrase "Yes, I'd be happy to" crossed my lips, the phrase, "Against the rules" rattled around in my brain. Wasn't it against the rules? Yet it was the *theology* professor who had asked for my help. If she was asking, surely it was okay. But then, she had a reputation for being something of a rebel!

Together, we raised the Body of Christ high over the altar. Together, we pressed gently, and, with a light snap, the circular wafer broke just about evenly along the vertical crease. I paused behind the altar, while the priest called, "Alleluia! Christ our Passover is sacrificed for us," and then quietly moved back to my seat in the first row during the congregation's response.

Though I've been a priest for many years now and have broken the bread at the altar thousands of times, it is the image of this shared fraction that most often springs to mind when I hear the words, "The Body of Christ." It is not the fresh, first-timeness of feeling the wafer give way that is so impressed in my being. It is the uneven tenuousness of breaking it in concert with another's hand, the joint nature of the act, the recollection of Jesus' death once *for all.*

As a result of this singular, powerful experience of shared breaking, when I stand behind the altar and touch the eucharistic bread, I often imagine someone else has joined me at the altar. As I enact Christ's Body breaking, my heart pounds an extra beat as I experience the tearing, the fragmenting, at once so powerfully devastating and transforming. Surely, it would be good and right for this—not just the consuming, but also the breaking—to be shared.

I think it was a catechist in my adult Confirmation class in Oregon who told me a bit of eucharistic lore I have not heard since: "Once the bread is consecrated and becomes the Body of Christ, every bit of it is meant to be consumed by those present, so that the Body of Christ is made whole again in the gathered community." If this is true, if the Body of Christ is made whole in all of us together, how can it be right for only one of us to do the breaking? Since the Body of Christ is broken *for* all of us, why should it not be broken *by* all of us?

These days, as church attendance declines and we Episcopalians scramble to discern what we can do to reignite the vitality of our life together, we talk a great deal about the ministry of all the baptized. Yet there are many things—things that are central to church life—that lay people are not allowed to do, to touch.

Recently, I have been wondering: Would it change us—how would it change us—if the priest stopped breaking the bread alone? What if, Sunday by Sunday, each time we gathered for communion, someone stepped forward from the congregation during the prayers and reached up and helped. Break. The Body of Christ.

"...Therefore let us keep the feast. Alleluia."

Janet Waggoner is an Episcopal priest from the Diocese of Oregon who, after serving parishes in Connecticut for over a decade, is now serving in the Diocese of Fort Worth as interim pastor in a Lutheran congregation. Janet facilitates transformation in the lives of individuals and church communities through education, art, conciliation, and intergenerational connections. She is a board member of WIKS-USA, an organization that partners with Kenyans to provide quality education for underprivileged children. She is the mother of two children and wife of a theology professor.

An Unexpected Answer

I will cry aloud to God;
I will cry aloud,
and he will hear me.

— PSALM 77,
THE BOOK OF COMMON PRAYER, P. 693

I HAVE ENJOYED, above many other sports, baseball. Not watching baseball, but playing it. I was around seven or eight years old when I entered the minor leagues.

It was the second game of my first season, we were down by four runs, and I was up to bat. The pitcher threw the ball. I swung, and missed. The ball was thrown a second time. I swung, and missed again. My coach called me over, gave me a three-second pep talk, and pushed me back up to the plate. As he walked away, the coach called out one last time: "Do whatever you can. I know that you can hit the ball!"

So I stepped up to the plate and took the metal bat in my hands. You see, I had actually never hit a baseball except for on a tee. So I felt kind of scared. I was scared of failing, and I didn't want to let my team or my coach down. And then I did something I did rarely, except at church: I put the feeling into prayer. It was a short prayer, asking to hit the ball for my coach, and for my team.

When I swung, the ball went flying to third base. I was so surprised that I did not start running until my coach shouted at me. I took off, but not in enough time to reach the base. But that was okay, because God had heard me, and answered my call.

This might seem like a petty, silly little thing, but that day, my view of God and myself changed. It might have been a small change, but small things can sometimes be very important. Astronaut Neil Armstrong said, "That's one small step for man, one giant leap for mankind." A single step may be of no consequence in the everyday world. But a step on the moon is history. Hitting the baseball was the same thing for me that day. To a stranger who had not seen me trying to hit the ball, it might look like nothing. But to me, it was a sign.

When I prayed to God before I hit the baseball, he heard me. And he answered me. God always answers, and that time, God chose to answer by letting me hit the ball. Sometimes he answers us in different ways than we expect. God could have answered by letting me hit a home run, by my team winning the game, or by my father taking me out for a treat. Instead, he answered in a very inconspicuous way by just letting me hit the ball. Not for my selfish use, but so I could be better enlightened on my concept of prayer.

In the end, I guess, what God taught me in that moment wasn't really about hitting the baseball or scoring runs. It wasn't even about that famous saying that, "It's not whether you win or lose; it's how you play the game." Instead, God taught me about prayer. Before I hit the ball, my view of prayer was that you pray when you want something, or when you follow the words in the worship bulletin in church. When I could not hit the ball, I wanted something so I prayed to God for help.

Hitting the ball after I prayed to God might not seem like a big deal, but to me it proved that people do not pray to God to get what they want, but so they can talk to him. We pray to God because he listens, and he answers back. This incident opened my eyes, and now I find myself seeing more of God's answers to prayers everywhere I look.

All we have to do is listen to God, and his answers give us what we need.

Edward Michael Naish is a seventh grader from Lexington, Kentucky. He is a member of the Christ Church Cathedral Boys Choir and the youth group. In addition to writing, Michael enjoys reading, playing the piano and viola, and swimming. He hopes to continue his passion for music and writing in high school and college.

Out of Emptiness

Almighty God, who hast knit together thine elect
in one communion and fellowship,
in the mystical body of thy Son Christ our Lord:
Grant, we beseech thee, to thy whole Church
in paradise and on earth,
thy light and thy peace. Amen.

— *The Book of Common Prayer*, p. 480

As a seminarian preparing to become a priest, I told myself that I had given my life to Christ to do as he wanted, and that I was ready to follow wherever he would call me. I was being prepared to totally follow.

I was at St. Luke's in Atlanta taking a course in Clinical Pastoral Education during the summer of 1982, working in the soup kitchen that fed about six hundred people daily, mostly homeless men. On Wednesdays, we celebrated the Eucharist after serving these men. One of those Wednesdays, as I knelt at the communion rail, someone signaled to me that I had an emergency call. My father was dying, and I needed to return to Texas right away.

I left immediately, but when I landed and saw my sister and two brothers at the airport, I knew I had not arrived in time. My father was a key figure in my life. He had more faith in me than I could ever have. As far as he was concerned, there was nothing I could not accomplish if I set my mind to it. I felt as though my grounding had been removed from my life.

After the funeral, I returned to Sewanee, Tennessee, and four months later, I answered the phone. My younger sister was crying and saying, "Mother is dead." I did not comprehend what was happening, so I asked who it was and assured her that I would call her right back. Then it hit me: my mother was dead.

After her funeral, I returned to Tennessee again with a very heavy heart and a profound sense of loss and emptiness. I spoke to my spiritual friend, and she suggested going to the Abbey of Gethsemani in Kentucky. I wrote to inquire about a retreat. One of the sisters at Bethany Spring, the retreat center connected with the Abbey, wrote back: "I read your letter, and you have had a tremendous number of losses in your life. You are welcome to come and spend a week with us, but as I read your letter, I sensed a need to tell you that I truly believe that only God can help you."

I packed a bag and drove to Gethsemani. I checked in and went to my assigned room. Dinner was shared in silence. The next day I met with the sister in charge. She explained that she would give me three lessons from Scripture to read each day, and we would spend one hour per day sharing verbally. The rest of the time was to be spent in silence in the presence of God.

First day: I read, we spoke, I prayed, I walked around the grounds. I fell asleep.

Second day: I read, we spoke, I prayed, I walked around the grounds. I fell asleep praying.

Third day: I read, we spoke, I prayed and meditated on a lesson about our treasure being in a clay vessel, and I began to question what this might be saying to me. Was I the clay vessel? What was the treasure within that clay vessel? And most of all, what if there was nothing in this clay vessel that bore my name?

I walked over to the place called the Garden of Gethsemani. As I walked the little hill, I came upon a gigantic statue of Peter, James, and John sleeping. Then I walked a little farther, and I saw an outstanding statue, a bronze of Jesus kneeling, with his head lifted up and his hands covering his face. He looked as though he were in agony. I sensed that because agony is what I was experiencing at that moment.

I slowly got closer to the statue of Jesus and found myself embracing him for what seemed an eternity. I cried, held him, questioned him, cried some more, embraced him even more, and then experienced a deep sense of fatigue. I stepped back and sat on a small chair that had probably been placed there so people could meditate. Instead, I fell asleep under a tree, and a few hours later, leaves fell on my face, awakening me with their flutter and their softness as the branches above shaded me from the sun.

I stood and walked away after touching Jesus and the statue of Peter, James, and John. I went back to Bethany Spring, where I was staying. After a silent supper, I went to my room, and as I walked into the room, I was overwhelmed with a deep sense of fear. I turned toward the door to make sure that it was locked. No sooner had I locked myself in the room than arose a sense of panic that what I was afraid of was in the room with me.

Then the words from the Burial of the Dead: Rite I in *The Book of Common Prayer* (p. 480) suddenly came to me. "Almighty God, who hast knit together thine elect in one communion and fellowship, in the mystical body of thy son Christ our Lord..." I was not alone; I was in the very midst of the communion of saints, which included my mother and father. I felt absolutely exposed and vulnerable in their presence. I continued to ask myself: why this sense of such fear to the point of panic?

Then I remembered the Scripture I had meditated on that day about our treasure being hidden in earthen vessels.

Could there be a treasure hidden in this vessel called Carmen? Could I dare to go inward? What if there was nothing there? What if all that I told myself I believed as a woman of faith was just external? The more I questioned, the more the panic and the fear grew. This struggle continued until I was too exhausted to fight it any more.

I journeyed inward into this clay vessel named Carmen, and there I found a profound emptiness. The treasure was literally emptiness. And yet in finding my own emptiness I found an abundance of every-thingness. In my emptiness I found a profound wholeness. I found what I can today only describe as God. I found my identity as one interlaced with the communion of saints and God all in one.

I knew my life was changing, and I was not in control of the change that was happening. As I spun deeper and deeper, I understood that the treasure within had nothing to do with my efforts but totally with the presence of God that I had never realized. How then was I to live?

Ever since I asked myself that question all those years ago, whenever I think I have become a changed person, it is as though I have only just begun to get a glimpse of what being changed might mean. There are days when it is quite clear, and then there are days when I barely comprehend what this was—and is—about. What I think, what I know, is that at my age of seventy-one, someone, the one I call God, continues to be present and active and a profound life-changing reality in my life.

———————■———————

Carmen Guerrero was born in Texas to a Mexican mother and Italian father, and reared in a fully bilingual, multicultural family and environment. Being raised in a government housing project in San Antonio, Texas, provided her with a wide and profound understanding of justice, economic struggles, and a vision for the difference between what is and what ought to be in our society. A priest for over half her life, Carmen has served in a variety of ministries couched in her commitment to compassion, justice, and the presence of God in the lives of all. She is currently semi-retired and works part-time for the Diocese of Arizona as their canon for peace, justice, and multicultural ministry. She and her husband, Paul, have a garden and an orchard, and volunteer on issues of justice, immigration, antiracism, and hunger, when they are not swimming in their backyard pool.

Workshop One

Opening Prayer

God, as we gather together to discuss our own stories, help us to remember the many ways that you tell your story to us: in biblical teachings, in the apostles' fellowship, in our eucharistic liturgies, and in the prayers we offer. May we know your presence in these acts, and, discovering your heart and your love, may we grow in confidence to share that love with the world. Amen.

Questions for Discussion

1. Eva Suarez writes about how her relationship to the Lord's Prayer deepened and changed over time, offering comfort and insight in different ways. What is prayer to you, and what is its purpose? Is there a prayer that you often pray, and if so, why? How has your relationship to that prayer changed over time? How has it changed you and your relationship to God?

2. In the story that Marilyn McCord Adams shares, Pat is a woman whose commitment to Christ's teachings and fellowship knows no bounds. Marilyn explains that Pat shares her love for the wisdom of Jesus through spiritual conversations with others. How have you participated in the apostles' teaching and fellowship? How has it changed your faith life and your relationship to God?

3. Janet Waggoner describes a moment that changed her understanding of the Eucharist. Has there been an experience where the Eucharist changed you or your understanding of the Church?

4. At the end of his story, Edward Michael Naish writes that, "All we have to do is listen to God and his answers give us what we need." Yet Michael also acknowledges that sometimes what we need is not what we expect to receive. How do you make sense of this incongruity? Does it ring true for you?

5. Carmen Guerrero describes how, in many ways, the purpose of the prayers, liturgies, and the apostles' teaching and fellowship experiences is to empower us to be the hands of God in the world. How are these storytellers the hands of God in the world? How can you learn from their experiences in order to be the hands of God in the world?

Prompts for Writing Your Spiritual Story

1. The Catechism in *The Book of Common Prayer* (pp. 843-862) says that we commonly offer prayer for these reasons: to express our adoration of God, to praise God, in thanksgiving for the good things that happen to us, in penitence for our sins, for the purpose of oblation or offering ourselves to God's service, in intercession for the needs of others, and to petition or ask for the things that we need.

Recall a moment that you prayed to God. Which— if any of these—were you praying for? How did God respond and how did that response change your relationship with God? How did it change you?

2. Liturgy has always been important to Episcopalians, and today we continue to gather in worship to break bread and to pray together. Recall a worship service that was meaningful to you. How did your faith life change as a result of that worship service? How did your relationship with God and the wider community change as a result?

3. Christian formation is an important way that we grow in our understanding of the apostles' teaching and fellowship, yet we are also formed by experiences outside our churches' walls. Recall a moment when you were formed in faith, either through church formation or through another formative experience. How did this experience empower you to be God's hands in the world?

After you've selected a prompt, describe the event or moment and its significance to you in a story of a thousand words or less.

Closing Prayer

God, we ask your blessing upon us as we seek to hear the stories of our tradition, stories of the apostles' teaching and fellowship, stories of breaking bread. May the wisdom of these stories increase our own, so that we may share with richness stories from our own lives. May these stories empower us and others to be God's hands in the world, working to make a new and abundant creation for all. Amen.

Visit **spiritualstories.forwardmovement.org**
to read more stories—and, if you'd like, share your own.

Returning

Celebrant

*Will you persevere in resisting evil,
and, whenever you fall into sin,
repent and return to the Lord?*

People

I will, with God's help.

GREGORY ORRIN BREWER

Crossing the Yellow Line

Lord, we pray that your grace may always
precede and follow us,
that we may continually be given to good works;
through Jesus Christ our Lord,
who lives and reigns with you and the Holy Spirit,
one God, now and for ever. Amen.

— *THE BOOK OF COMMON PRAYER, P. 234*

I DRIVE INTO THE PARRAMORE neighborhood of Orlando, leaving the relative uniformity of comfortable suburbia for the other part of town. Parramore is poverty-stricken and mostly African American. There is no gentrification here. It has never been a nice neighborhood. If you ask a local for a description of Parramore, the one word you always hear is dangerous.

Driving into Parramore in my late-model sedan, I am slightly uncomfortable, even though this is not a new experience. I have been in these neighborhoods before, neighborhoods that we call the other part of town. My doors are locked, and I'm listening to the radio as a distraction from the gray monotony of boarded-up buildings and small knots of young people hanging out on street corners.

I am on my way to visit IDignity, an interchurch effort that provides photo identifications free of charge for those who don't have them. Most of the clients don't have a home, and, as any social worker will tell you, without a home, you can't get a photo ID, and without a photo ID, the likelihood of getting any state or federal aid is nil. Without a photo ID, you do not qualify.

The need is enormous. IDignity opens their center at ten in the morning, and people line up outside the building as early as 4:00 a.m. By the time I arrive, the line stretches way beyond the building. Most of the people in line are quietly staring down at the sidewalk. Yellow caution tape cordons off those waiting from the rest of the sidewalk.

I park my car. Lock it. I make my way into a side entrance, away from those waiting in line, to meet the people in charge of the program. These volunteers are unflaggingly cheerful, as if they take comfort in knowing that they do something meaningful and important. I am warmly welcomed, and we start the tour. I am a tourist, you know. I know almost nothing of what it means to live in Parramore, much less to be homeless. And while as a bishop I am used to visiting different churches each week, there is something different about touring this place: Here I find myself separated by the home I live in and the yellow tape at the building. Here, I feel myself the outsider, and it's uncomfortable, though I realize that feeling like an outsider is what the people on the other side of the yellow tape must experience all of the time.

A cheerful volunteer leads me to the line, and I shake hands with clients who are already inside the building. I am on one side of the caution tape, and they are on the other. Some people look up and shake hands. Most people do not. Few make eye contact. I am a bishop, and for better or worse, I am used to my purple bishop's shirt signifying something. It means nothing to them. I am only a tourist, and they know it.

Then a woman speaks up. She has noticed my shirt color and the cross around my neck. "Can you pray for my friend?" she asks.

"Sure," I say.

She steps aside to reveal another woman, smaller in stature, leaning against the wall of the building. I hear that this woman is not well, has a child, and has been waiting in line for hours. Without thinking, I am under the yellow line of caution tape and standing beside the woman. Quickly, I am surrounded by people who are now watching and waiting to see what I am going to say.

I notice an unexpected well of emotion rising inside me. I am in an enclosure of human brokenness, and what I have to offer seems so small. But I start to pray, first inside, asking God for words; first silently and then out loud. For a very brief moment, we, together, are the Church, praying for a woman with great need and little hope. God is wonderfully present. When the prayer is over, there are a few smiles—the first I've seen.

God was, and is, present on the other side of the yellow line.

Gregory Orrin Brewer is the fourth Bishop of the Diocese of Central Florida. Prior to serving there, he was rector of Calvary-St. George's Church, a multicultural, multiracial parish with landmarked historic buildings in downtown Manhattan. He has published articles in a variety of venues, including *The Anglican Digest*, and is an Eagle Scout who enjoys sailing, cooking for friends, and classical and jazz music. He lives with his wife and three children in Orlando, Florida.

Darkness Is Not Dark

*If I say, "Surely the darkness will cover me,
and the light around me turn to night,"
darkness is not dark to you, O Lord;
the night is as bright as the day;
darkness and light to you are both alike.*

— Psalm 139:10-11,
The Book of Common Prayer, p. 110

Six months after the destruction of the World Trade Center, I finally found the courage to accept the invitation from my bishop to visit the site with a group of young people from Los Angeles. I dressed as a priest with my black shirt and white collar. I was expected to minister to the young people—to be prepared to help them deal with the traumatic encounter. All the while, I was the one who was in need of pastoral care. I'd already had many opportunities to go to the World Trade Center site in previous trips to New York to visit my mother and to work with the churches in the area, but I had avoided it time and again.

So there I was with a group of young people at St. Paul's Chapel, the Episcopal church closest to the World Trade Center. The miracle at St. Paul's Chapel was that not a single windowpane was broken when the buildings fell, even though three feet of debris piled up in the cemetery behind the church. St. Paul's had been a place of rest and worship for the firefighters and workers at the site. The walls of the church were covered with banners and letters of support and prayers sent by children across the country and the world. It was a holy place. I felt out of place. While the young people listened to an orientation by one of the clergy working there, I wandered off to look at the letters and art around the sanctuary.

A fireman tapped me on my shoulder. I looked up and saw a broad, smiling face. He extended his hand to me; I held it and immediately felt the calluses of his palm and fingers. "You're a priest, right?"

"Yes." I did not know how to react, so I did the standard thing. "I'm with that group of young people from Los Angeles."

"I thought you should have this." He reached into his pocket with his other hand and pulled out a piece of granite. He handed it to me. It was covered with dust. "This is a piece of the World Trade Center."

In my shock, all I could say was, "Thank you."

He then told me that he was a retired fireman. When he heard about the attack, he came to volunteer, and he had been on-site five days a week ever since. He had been digging every day, recovering the remains of those who died. He spoke as one who had seen the horror of the destruction but in a calm, you-do-what-you-have-to-do manner. As he spoke, I felt my fear and apprehension retreating. I sensed that I was coming back down to the ground of reality. At that moment, I realized I had accepted the piece of the World Trade Center that he gave me. I felt my palm and fingers being edged by the roughness of the granite from the tight clutch of my hand. I released my hand and looked at the stone. The dust from the stone stuck to the sweat of my palm. I realized that the dust was not just dust from the building. It was partly the ashes of the people who died. I cried.

"Thanks for giving this to me." I looked at him through my tears. "This really means a lot to me." I then introduced him to some of the young people from my group. They asked him questions and took pictures of his hands.

I held the piece of granite in my palm all through the Eucharist later that day. I cried and prayed for the dead. I cried and gave thanks for the courage and dedication of the people doing the daunting recovery work. I cried and gave thanks to God for letting me know that even in the most devastating moment, at the heart of destruction, there is still redemption and hope. As I looked at the faces of the young people in my group, I thanked God for community in this time of sadness, anger, and uncertainty.

Later that day, after the worship service, I saw that same fireman sitting in a back pew with another fireman, talking quietly. I said to myself, "What an angel!"

At the crossing of my own fear and my role as a pastor, I was tempted to hold on to my prescribed role and behavior as a priest, ignoring my own need and the needs of the others. I was tempted to not allow myself to feel the pain of those who suffered and died. Instead, an angel ministered to me—this retired fireman who gave me a piece of the World Trade Center. The message I received was: "You do what you have to do with all the mixed emotion and confused passions. You do the best that you can based on what you know with all its fear and apprehension. That's okay with God. You might make mistakes; you might be broken down; you might even unknowingly hurt another; but in the end, God will send an angel to minister to you. You are blessed, you are fallen, and you are redeemable as a beloved child of God."

(Modified from an excerpt from *The Word at the Crossing: Living the Good News in a Multicontextual Community* by Eric H. F. Law, St. Louis: Chalice Press, 2003.)

Eric H. F. Law, an Episcopal priest, is the founder and executive director of the Kaleidoscope Institute, an organization that works to create inclusive and sustainable churches and communities. For more than twenty years, he has provided transformative and comprehensive training and resources for churches and ministries in all of the major church denominations in the United States and Canada. He is the author of seven books including *The Wolf Shall Dwell with the Lamb* (Chalice Press, 1993) and his latest, *Holy Currencies: Six Blessings for Sustainable Missional Ministries* (Chalice Press, 2013). He writes a weekly blog, *The Sustainist: Spirituality for Sustainable Communities in a Networked World,* which can be found at http://ehflaw.typepad.com/blog/.

Pray for Hobie

The Holy Eucharist, the principal act of Christian worship on the Lord's Day and other major Feasts, and Daily Morning and Evening Prayer, as set forth in this Book, are the regular services appointed for public worship in this Church.

— *THE BOOK OF COMMON PRAYER, P. 13*

I WANT TO INTRODUCE YOU to someone I met one day after church. It was a brief encounter, probably no more than five minutes from beginning to end. And it changed my life profoundly—and, I hope, forever.

I was in my last assignment as a priest before becoming a bishop, serving a fairly large parish, St. Bartholomew's in Atlanta. St. Bartholomew's had a well-deserved reputation for being concerned about outreach and social justice ministries. Part of the parish history is that during the Civil Rights Movement, the members were known to cancel coffee hour in order to board chartered buses and join demonstrations for school integration at the state capitol downtown. St. Bartholomew's started the first shelter for homeless families in Atlanta by turning its Sunday School classrooms into bedrooms on Sunday afternoon and transforming them back into classrooms early on Sunday morning. It hosted the local outreach ministry for emergency assistance. Because of all these things, it had a constant flow of people who were poor for one reason or another.

And that is why our community had a very important rule: Sunday was reserved for worship. And so on Sunday we would not consider—under any circumstances—requests for help with rent, or transportation, or paying the utility bill, or whatever. We provided assistance on every other day of the week, but on Sunday, we worshiped, which is something else St. Bartholomew's was—and still is—quite good at. The reason for the policy was the concern that if word spread that we were open for the business of helping people with such needs on Sunday, we would be absolutely overrun and not able to attend to the main business of the day, which was to pray.

One particular Sunday, I was greeting people at the door after the service when an usher came up to me and reported a man was asking to see the pastor. When someone unknown shows up and asks for the pastor, it usually means one thing. I glanced over my shoulder. Sure enough, the man looked homeless. I told the usher to tell the man I would be with him in a minute. I did not mean "in a minute" literally. I meant "when I get around to it." I actually meant "when I get around to it, and I hope you'll be gone by then." I greeted everyone coming out of the door. I greeted everyone else I could think of. I went back to the sacristy to greet the altar guild. I went into the kitchen to greet the breakfast cooks. And when there was no one else, I went to face this person I knew was going to ask for a handout and whom I knew I was going to turn away empty-handed with instructions to come back Monday. He had waited patiently for me.

When I found the man, I asked, in a tone that I'm sure conveyed my implicit message, "What can I do for you?" I did not ask him to come to my office. I did not even invite him into a more private place than the spot where he was standing in the foyer. I just asked, "What can I do for you?" because I knew he was going to ask for something, and I, in turn, was going to say no.

What he asked instead was, "Pray for Hobie." I stood convicted without being judged. When I recovered, I invited him to come into the church with me. And then I asked, "Who is Hobie?" He patted his own chest. And mine was cracked open. And we stood there in the church, with nearly everyone else gone, with my arm around this stranger, and we prayed for Hobie. I think I did most of the talking because I knew I had a number of things I needed to say to God. Hobie just listened, or maybe Hobie was praying on his own. I hope Hobie might have been praying for me.

And at that point, another usher came up to ask one of those all-important questions clergy hear on a Sunday morning like "where are the bank deposit slips?" or "to whom should the altar flowers be delivered?" or "what should I do about the toilet overflowing in the bathroom?" I excused myself from Hobie to deal with whatever it was, which now seemed more an annoyance distracting me from Hobie than an excuse for ignoring him, but I promised I would be right back.

When I returned, however, Hobie was gone. Vanished. Disappeared. It was as if he had never been there at all. I looked around the church for him. Nowhere. I went out into the churchyard. Nowhere. I went and looked up and down the street. Nowhere. Just gone.

It was not so much a lesson, I suppose, as it was a reminder—and perhaps a warning. The lesson, in truth, I had already learned long before. This is the lesson: As strange as this is going to sound, one of the things that really matters in life is being in relationship with people who are poor because it is in them that we meet Jesus, just as profoundly and just as truly as in the

Eucharist. They have everything to do with God in the flesh, concretely, tangibly. It is best not to forget that. It is not about helping the poor. It is about worshiping God in spirit and in truth.

Stacy Sauls is a bishop and chief operating officer of The Episcopal Church. He coordinates the work of the Church's mission program, communication, finance, and administration duties while assisting Presiding Bishop Katharine Jefferts Schori in her role as chief executive officer. He is an ex-officio member of The Episcopal Church's Executive Council and an active member of the board of Episcopal Relief & Development. Prior to this call, Bishop Sauls served as Bishop of The Diocese of Lexington, Kentucky. He is a past member of The Episcopal Church's Executive Council and has served on the Standing Commission on World Mission, the Standing Commission on Constitution and Canons, the Budgetary Funding Task Force, and the Joint Committee on the Philippines Covenant, of which he was co-chair. He is also active with mission projects in Japan.

Workshop Two

Opening Prayer

God, we see the effects of sin and evil in the world and in our lives in so many ways, some evident, some unforeseen. Help us to know when evil and sin surround us, and help us to persevere in resisting their power. Yet, in the moments when we feel overcome by their strength, help us to know that you forgive all, redeem all, and welcome us with open arms. May we feel your presence in the pain and suffering in our lives until we know that all is redeemed, and that this is a message we can spread, with confidence, to a world that longs so desperately for hope and healing. Amen.

Questions for Discussion

1. *The Book of Common Prayer* states that "Sin is the seeking of our own will instead of the will of God, thus distorting our relationship with God, with other people, and with all creation" (Catechism, p. 848). What about this definition of sin resonates with you? What, if anything, do you object to in this definition?

2. Do you think there is a relationship between sin and evil? If so, how do you understand it? Do you see sin in the three stories in this section? Do you see evil?

3. *The Book of Common Prayer* defines redemption as "the act of God which sets us free from the power of evil, sin, and death" (Catechism, p. 849). What about this definition of redemption resonates with you? Is there anything about it that you do not like, and if so, why?

4. Where do you see redemption in the three stories in this section?

5. Does each author seem to share a similar understanding of redemption, or do they understand this concept differently?

Prompts for Writing Your Spiritual Story

1. Recall a moment where you felt the presence of sin in your life. What was that moment like, and did you experience any kind of redemption in its aftermath? How did that change your relationship with God and your faith life?

2. Recall an experience of evil. Think about what this moment felt like in your body and any physical sensations that accompanied it. How did this event affect you psychologically and spiritually? Try to recall whether and how God was present in that moment.

3. Sometimes it takes a long time to feel any kind of resolution or redemption in the aftermath of sin and evil. Pick a moment in your life when you have not felt that resolution. How did this moment affect and continue to affect your faith life? Do you hold hope that it will eventually be redeemed? How did it impact your perception of God? Does it continue to spiritually challenge you, or are you at peace with it?

After you've selected a prompt, describe the event or moment and its significance to you in a story of a thousand words or less.

Closing Prayer

God, you tell us that when darkness covers us, you will surround us with light. You assure us that you will make night as bright as day. May the sure hope of your grace and redemption always be in our hearts, as we meet the challenges of sin and evil. In all that we do, help us to know that you will light the way. Amen.

Visit **spiritualstories.forwardmovement.org**
to read more stories—and, if you'd like, share your own.

Proclaiming

Celebrant

*Will you proclaim
by word and example
the Good News of God in Christ?*

People

I will, with God's help.

Espwa fé Viv
Hope Gives Life

Versicle   *Let not the needy,*
             O Lord, be forgotten;

Response   *Nor the hope of the poor be taken away.*

— THE BOOK OF COMMON PRAYER, P. 98

It was a little more than one year after the 2010 earthquake when I joined three other missioners from a parish in Georgia for my first trip to rural Haiti.

Before that mission trip, I had witnessed poverty in West Africa and Brazil. Several years prior, I'd led a mission trip to an Episcopal girls' school in Liberia, and more than twenty years ago, when I worked in São Paulo, I had taken a trip to Bahía, in northeast Brazil.

But Haiti was different.

The first thing I saw—and smelled—when I stepped out of Toussaint Louverture International Airport in Port-au-Prince was this: just across the street, a sea of tarps—white plastic, blue plastic, gray plastic—held together by sticks and string, side-by-side in the blazing sun.

Only seconds later, I saw the clothes drying in the narrow paths between tents. People of all ages bathing right out in the open, with dirty water. Piles and piles of rubble. Goats, chickens, and feral dogs running everywhere. Mounds and mounds of trash. Gutters overflowing with open sewage.

It was the closest thing I've ever seen to hell on earth.

Yes, yes—before this mission trip I had read up on Haiti's extreme poverty. I'd seen the images of the utter and complete devastation wrought by the earthquake.

I understood that daily life in Haiti was tormented by the search for work and finding ways to earn money for food, separation from family members, sicknesses not found in other levels of society, infant malnutrition and mortality, unfair prices for the basics. I understood all that.

But only after riding in the back of a truck for the three-hour journey from Port-au-Prince to the mountain village of Trouin, only when I came face-to-face with it, did I begin to grasp the sheer size of the problem.

"How on earth is it possible for these people to have any hope at all?" I asked myself.

On that trip, Haitians told me their stories about how their lives had changed since the earthquake. And as I listened, what made those stories unforgettable— what made them so powerful—is what I found in the faces, gestures, and words of those storytellers.

Instead of tears, I found laughter.

Instead of grief, I found joy.

Instead of despair, I found hope.

One night, after a full day of work in Trouin, followed by a delicious dinner of rice, mangoes, and fried plantains, I was deep in after-dinner conversation with Mme. Georgette, in whose house our mission team stayed.

I could tell from worshiping daily with Georgette that she was a woman of deep wisdom, of a firm and sure faith. That question about the hope of the poor had been nagging at my heart ever since I had arrived in Haiti, so I decided to ask Georgette about it.

My flashlight was starting to lose power, but I just had to have an answer before I turned in for the night. "Georgette," I asked, "please tell me...how is it that you, the people of Haiti, with all of the problems there are here, all of the difficulties you face every day, all of the... well, how is it that you manage to have any hope at all?"

Georgette cradled my face in her weathered hands. Her eyes met mine as she took a deep breath. "Père

Kate," she replied, "when you are on the path, and you fall down, you can always get up."

"It is in the getting up," Georgette continued, "that we have hope. Haiti may fall down, but we always hope. And we know that we will always rise again. In the rising, there is hope."

Could there be any clearer explanation of the resurrection than that?

"In the rising, there is hope."

"And, Père Kate," she smiled, "as we say here in Haiti, *Espwa fè viv*—'Hope gives life.'"

———————■———————

Kate Bryant, an Episcopal priest, has a passion for outreach ministry, pastoral leadership, and an understanding of what makes churches grow and thrive as the body of Christ. A graduate of Berkeley Divinity School at Yale, Kate was a Canterbury Scholar in 2005. She received a B.A. from The Johns Hopkins University. Kate is a priest associate of the Society of St. Margaret, an Episcopal convent. A cradle Episcopalian, she is a native of Washington, D. C.

Bo Cox

Balloons and Heaven

*On the third day he rose again
in accordance with the Scriptures;
he ascended into heaven
and is seated at the right hand of the Father.*

— THE NICENE CREED,
THE BOOK OF COMMON PRAYER, P. 327

EVERYONE HEARD HIM COMING before they saw him. The doors swung violently open, and a young man came rushing through, swinging a homemade weapon made from a pair of D batteries wrapped inside a doubled-up pair of tube socks. In the hallway was a water fountain that he'd torn from the wall and a handful of medical staff, hands to their mouths and eyes as big as saucers.

Sometimes you see things like this, working in a state-run psych hospital that is often a last resort for people in desperate need.

When Two or Three Are Gathered

This young man was in that kind of need. He ran to the end of another hallway, where he backed into a corner and dared anyone to get close. Anytime someone approached, he would swing the sock and knock holes in the wall to illustrate his potential for violence.

I recognized him. He and I had built some rapport, so I headed down the hallway toward him. After asking him if I could talk to him, I sat on the floor, and after a few minutes, he gave up the weapon and went back to his ward.

Later that evening, I got a knock on my office door.

"Can I talk to you?" the young man asked.

"Sure," I told him. "What's up?"

"Well," he began and tears filled his eyes. "Tomorrow is Mother's Day and, well, I need you to help me get a card to my mom. She died last year, and, uh, I made her a Mother's Day card this afternoon."

"That's awfully nice," I began, trying to understand what my role could possibly be and beginning to glimpse a fraction of this young man's pain.

"Would you get me a helium balloon?" he asked. "I know she's in heaven, and I want to send my card to her."

All my theological beliefs came rushing forward, and I wanted to tell him that a helium-filled balloon couldn't get to heaven any more than a rocket ship or a kite and that his heartfelt, homemade card had already traveled there because of the love he put into it.

Instead, I told him I'd be right back.

I went to the store and got a Mother's Day balloon filled with helium. When he saw me, I realized from the look on his face that he hadn't expected me to return.

"You ready?" I asked.

He nodded his head, and we headed out into the courtyard.

He tied his card to the balloon with shaking hands and released it into the air.

We stood there, watching it get smaller and smaller, when he said, "Hey, Bo, can I ask you a question?"

"What is it?" I said.

"How far up will my balloon go?" he asked.

"It'll go as far as you need it to."

Bo Cox lives in Norman, Oklahoma, with his wife, Debb, two dogs, and five cats. When he's not playing in the woods with them, he spends his time playing games with people who find themselves in the psychiatric hospital where he works as a recreational therapist. Bo has written for Forward Movement for almost twenty years, beginning with the contributions to *Forward Day by Day* that he first penned from prison in 1995. He is also the author of *God is Not in the Thesaurus: Stories from an Oklahoma Prison* (Forward Movement, 1999).

Blessing Jokita

*I lay my hands upon you
in the Name of our Lord and Savior Jesus Christ,
beseeching him to uphold you
and fill you with his grace,
that you may know the healing power of his love.*

— THE BOOK OF COMMON PRAYER, P. 456

MULI BWANJI.
Ndili bwino, kaya inu?
Ndili bwino.
Zikomo.
"Hi, how are you?"
"I'm well; how are you?"
"Fine."
"Thanks!"

Our group of eleven practiced this simple exchange in Chichewa over and over. We were on a "transformational journey" from our suburban church just north of New York City to the tiny, impoverished, nation of Malawi in central southeast Africa. I was the trip's spiritual leader, and Etta, a physician, was in charge of our itinerary. Our band of travelers included artists, teachers and students, an engineer, and several other medical professionals. We had been preparing for our trip for months and wanted, at the very least, to know enough of the language to be cordial once we got into the villages.

We were not on a mission trip. Our church was supporting an organization called Global AIDS Interfaith Alliance (GAIA) that does community-based HIV/AIDS care, education, and prevention in Malawi. Etta and I thought it might deepen our parish's investment in GAIA, and perhaps create more of a sense of partnership, if a group traveled to Malawi to see their work firsthand. We imagined ourselves as part ambassadors, part fact-finders, part witnesses to the gospel.

Our schedule was ambitious, and after five days we were on sensory overload. We'd been to countless village schools, hospitals, and gardens. We'd served at a feeding program for orphans, visited the only palliative care center in all Malawi, and spent hours at an infant crisis center holding critically ill babies.

Yet, in spite of the physical exhaustion that emerged from jet lag, culture shock, and exposure to human pain, we were mentally and spiritually alive with questions. Each evening we prayed and reflected on the day, wondering aloud what transformation really meant for us and for the people of Malawi. Did it matter that we were there? Could we do anything? The artists among us wanted to tell the story; the scientists wanted to fix things. And I, the priest, wanted answers too and found myself waiting for God to make an entrance and give me my longed-for "Aha" moment of clarity and purpose.

On day five of our trip, we traveled to the western edge of Malawi to meet Sister Agnes and her order of nuns. The sisters had built a school, hospital, and maternity clinic. They regularly traveled to provide medical care in remote areas, and after our tour Etta pressed Sister Agnes to take us into a village so that we might better comprehend the impact of HIV/AIDS on the poorest of the poor.

Illness and death at first seemed absent when our van arrived; the villagers greeted us with much singing and dancing. We formed a circle and began to greet one another.

Muli Bwanji!

Ndili bwino, kaya inu?

One of our travelers began telling stories to the children, another practiced the village dance, the local chief made a speech. The spirit was celebratory. Then, without fanfare, in groups of two or three, Sister Agnes led us into a small, dark hut to meet a woman named Jokita. I watched as members of our group entered the hut smiling and came out expressionless. I was the last to enter, and as I did, my stomach clenched, and the laughter and brightness of the world outside faded away.

The room was not much bigger than a king-sized bed. There were no lights, no windows; a thin mat covered the dirt floor. As my eyes adjusted, Sister Agnes whispered the story: Jokita's husband had died several years ago, but no one spoke the disease's dreaded name. Jokita was on an HIV drug regimen but continued to have symptoms, and she'd been hidden away, kept out of sight like so many others because of shame and stigma.

Jokita sat up on the mat, her face blank, her three young children crouched beside their mother's feet. I sank to my knees too. The village children outside the hut were clapping and singing, but these three children were motionless and silent. Inside the hut, the air was heavy and still, and the only sound was Jokita's dry cough.

I didn't know what to do, so I just sat there.

I sat and looked at Jokita. She seemed young and old at the same time. I prayed to God, *please help me know what to do*. Nobody moved or talked. I looked at the children whose eyes were glued to the floor. And then, without thinking, I took a breath and asked Sister Agnes to explain to Jokita that I was a priest from

America and would like to give her a blessing, if she didn't mind. Jokita raised her eyes and nodded. I slid closer and reached out to lay my hands on her. I touched her head and words flitted in my mind: *mother sister daughter woman*. In the words of our prayer book, I prayed for healing, for grace, for love to be poured into her. I stroked her damp skin and made the sign of the cross on her forehead. She didn't take her eyes off me, and her expression never changed. Tears fell down her cheeks. Her children sat silent and still.

Nothing happened. At least, nothing happened that I could point to and say "Aha." I just heard my own voice whispering words, I felt the warmth of our human touch, and I sensed God's presence with us in that hut. For an instant, the hard dirt floor beneath my knees became sacred ground.

Those brief moments in Jokita's hut left me humble and grateful. I might even say I was transformed and end the story there. But there is a postscript. One year later, I got word from Sister Agnes that Jokita was well. She wanted to thank "the holy woman from America who healed her." Jokita didn't credit the medicines we'd asked Sister Agnes to buy for her. As far as she was concerned, she had been made whole by God and restored to community by my healing hands.

For a year I had been praying for the repose of Jokita's soul, and I didn't quite know what to do with this new information. Jokita's healing wasn't about me,

I knew that. And healing isn't the same as curing; it takes many forms. Healing is its own transformational journey, and I'm on it along with everyone I know.

To this day, I can do no more than hold in my heart the mystery of one sacred exchange between a sick Malawian mother and the strange white woman from America. I can do no more than offer a prayer in Chichewa using one of the few words I remember, a word that is perhaps our only right response to God and to those who help transform us.

Zikomo.

Thank you.

Kate Malin is the rector of St. Anne's in-the-Fields in Lincoln, Massachusetts. Previously, she served as assistant at Christ Church, Bronxville, in New York. A graduate of The General Theological Seminary and Yale University, Kate is also the co-founder of Love's Harvest, a non-profit organization in Malawi that empowers the rural poor to grow nutritious food on their own land. Her sermons have been published in *The Old Testament in Christian Preaching* (The Episcopal Preaching Foundation, 2011).

JONATHAN A. MITCHICAN

Choking Up on Grace's Gift

Lord Jesus Christ, Son of the living God,
we pray you to set your passion, cross,
and death between your judgment and our souls,
now and in the hour of our death.

— THE BOOK OF COMMON PRAYER, P. 282

IT WAS A BOWL OF ARTIFICIALLY FLAVORED CEREAL that did it. At least, that is what I have decided in retrospect. Truth be told, it could have been a number of things I ate that day, but the bowl of cereal was the last thing I had at 10:30 p.m. before I went to bed. At 1:00 a.m., I was wide awake, gasping for air, with the sensation of my mouth filling uncontrollably with acid. My wife called the paramedics and less than an hour later I was lying on a bed in the emergency room at Mercy Fitzgerald Hospital with an IV in my arm.

What I would find out in the weeks after that night was that I have a condition called eosinophilic esophagitis. It is an allergic reaction that causes the throat to seize and inflame, in my case often making food get caught on the way down. This was not the first time that this condition had sent me to the emergency room, but it was by far the scariest because it seemed to come out of nowhere and have no explanation. I was not eating when it happened and it had come upon me when I was sleeping, making me afraid even to close my eyes. Once the condition was diagnosed, it was easily treated with medication and dietary changes, but I did not know that when I was lying in the hospital bed. All I knew then was I was in the hospital, alone because my wife had to stay home with our sleeping toddler, and I could very well be enjoying my last moments alive.

We live in a culture that denies death and tries to hide it from view, but as a priest I am not afforded the luxury of denial. I face death all the time, praying with people as they die and presiding over funerals. I get the call when someone is hit by a car or gets diagnosed with a terminal illness. On Ash Wednesday, I mark the foreheads of my parishioners with ashes and say, "Remember that you are dust and to dust you shall return." In all of that, I had come to think of death as a companion, an old friend who makes my sermons more interesting and gives my vocation as a priest some purpose. I had become numb to the truth of it, failing to realize that death is not a friend. Death is a horror, and one that we all must face.

Coming face to face with death that night, if only in my own mind, I was filled with fear. I realized that death will claim even me, that I am not special or somehow immune. Death will not be charmed away by my sarcasm or defeated by my intellect. When death wants me, death will have me, and there is not a damn thing I can do about it. All my fancy prayers and theologizing went out the window, and my prayer was reduced to a single word: "Help."

Eventually, the attack subsided, and I calmed down. I would sleep for a few minutes here and there, but I was constantly awakened. Every time I woke up, I reached for my Bible. I would turn to Paul's letter to the Romans and read a chapter before trying to sleep again. By the time I was released at 8:00 a.m. the next day, I had read through all sixteen chapters.

The Bible bores a lot of people, though I think that is because they do not know when to read it: Romans may sound like a bunch of antiquated words if you pick it up on any given Tuesday, but when you pick it up in a hospital bed when you think you might be dying, it is the most exciting and most relevant thing you have ever read.

There is no masking the reality of death in Romans. Paul knows what I came to learn, that death is everywhere, and it is a lot stronger than we will ever be.

But there is someone who is stronger even than death. "For if the many died through the one man's trespass," says Paul, "much more surely have the grace of God and the free gift in the grace of the one man, Jesus Christ, abounded for the many" (Romans 5:15). The world has known many great heroes, all of whom have died in the end. Jesus is the only one who faced death and lived. And in the process He opened the way, through faith in Him, for all of us to live.

I was already a Christian. I already knew this stuff. But somehow, being in that place, in that moment, the whole thing pierced my heart in a way that it never had before. Jesus died for me. And it goes way beyond that. He died for me without my asking Him to do it. He did not die for me because I am a good person who deserves to be loved. He died for me in spite of the fact that I am not a good person and that I am way more interested in myself than in God or other people. He died for me when I was at my weakest, at my lowest.

When I went up against death, there was nothing I could do. I was completely helpless. When He went up against death, it was the opposite. Death was totally powerless against Him. And because Jesus has chosen to give Himself to me, death is totally powerless against me too. "Where, O death, is your victory? Where, O death, is your sting?" (1 Corinthians 15:55).

God was with me that night, not in a feeling or in some sort of subjective, ethereal experience, but in his Word, in the promise that in Christ there is total forgiveness and total love. Love so strong that even death cannot touch it with a ten-foot pole.

It is one thing to preach grace. It is quite another to receive it. I still have moments when I fear death now, but when those moments come, I grab hold of the gospel and allow Jesus to show death the door. The truth of the matter is, I have been dead in sin since day one, but in Christ I will live forever. And when I contemplate even a fraction of that reality for more than a second, it becomes impossible not to shed tears of joy.

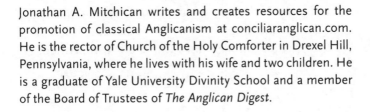

Jonathan A. Mitchican writes and creates resources for the promotion of classical Anglicanism at conciliaranglican.com. He is the rector of Church of the Holy Comforter in Drexel Hill, Pennsylvania, where he lives with his wife and two children. He is a graduate of Yale University Divinity School and a member of the Board of Trustees of *The Anglican Digest*.

My Call to Ministry in the Church

*O God, whom saints and angels delight
to worship in heaven:
Be ever present with your servants who seek
through art and music to perfect the praises
offered by your people on earth;
and grant to them even now glimpses of your beauty,
and make them worthy at length to behold it unveiled
for evermore; through Jesus Christ our Lord. Amen.*

— *THE BOOK OF COMMON PRAYER*, P. 819

MY PARENTS WOULD TELL ME THE STORY of when I was around two years old, and I would chase my godmother, Molly, around her house, shouting at the top of my lungs "Monoo!! Moonik!" which meant, "Molly, please play me some classical music!" The piece I wanted to hear, apparently, was Mendelssohn's incidental music to *A Midsummer Night's Dream.*

You see, I have been passionate about music for as long as I can remember.

This passion continued through my early childhood, and when I was just eight years old, I was invited to join the Portsmouth Cathedral Choir in the south of England. We sang four services a week and practiced every morning at the school that I attended. I was in heaven! I was awarded my surplice after only six months, instead of the normal one-year period.

But perhaps most importantly, being surrounded by the Word of God and singing those words must have made its way into my heart and soul, probably without my knowing or realizing. However, I believe part of me was subconsciously able to recognize His voice.

During my last year as a treble, my leadership skills were recognized when I was made Head Chorister. I then began to sing alto as my voice lowered with age.

Alto parts in music often have really wonderful harmony notes, which I'd sing with great gusto! Sadly, however, after two years, I found that this had damaged my voice, and I was advised to stop singing for a minimum of three years.

So, having been surrounded by the Word of God as set to music for over seven years, I found myself bereft of that source of inspiration and spiritual regeneration, though I may not have called it that at the time. Luckily, at least once a week I was able to enjoy the sung service of Evensong as provided by BBC Radio 3. It wasn't the same as actually singing the service, but it was something. (Even today, on Wednesdays, you can hear this service being broadcast live, both on the radio and on the Internet.)

It was on one of those Wednesdays, when I was about seventeen (some fifty years ago), that I received my call to the ministry that has occupied my life ever since. I remember distinctly sitting in the front room of my parents' house, listening to the radio broadcast of Evensong. I remember forming the question in my mind, "Lord, what is it you want me to do with my life?"

It was precisely at that point that I heard the "Prayer for Church Musicians and Artists" read as part of the prayers at the end of Evensong. It was a clear question-and-answer moment for me, coming directly from God. Since then, I have never looked back, even after a move of five thousand miles from my home country to ministry in, of all places, Ocala, Florida.

I have now been active in the ministry of church music almost continually since 1963, and have been in my present position as director of music since 1980. I plan to die here! I lead choirs and play the organ, guitar, trumpet, and piano. I also compose, teach, and lead workshops, festivals, and other groups around the country.

Inspired by hearing God's voice through music, I give my life to providing others the chance to hear it as well. I know beyond a shadow of a doubt that I am exactly where God wants me to be, and doing the work He wants me to do. May God give me the strength, wisdom, and good health to do His work to the best of my ability for many, many years to come.

Soli Deo Gloria!

Andrew Walker was born in 1955 and was raised and educated in England. As a child, he sang with the Portsmouth Cathedral Choir, and later earned a music degree from the University of London. He emigrated to the United States in 1977, and served first at Grace Episcopal Church in Ocala, Florida, and since 1980 as the director of music at St. Michael's Episcopal Church, Orlando. His music is published by the Royal School of Church Music and Paraclete Press, and he has also directed choir camps, Elderhostels, and workshops throughout the southeastern United States. At St. Michael's, he directs a very active music department of over ninety members of different ages and abilities. In 2009, he was elected to serve a term on the national board of directors of the American branch of The Royal School of Church Music, and is presently serving his second term as president. He is married to Gladys van den Berg, has three daughters, one granddaughter, and three grandsons.

Workshop Three

Opening Prayer

God, you call us to bring Good News to the world. Help us to see and experience the Good News in our own lives so that we may proclaim by word and example what you sent Christ to teach us: That your love can cause even evil and death to loosen their grasp on us. Amen.

Questions for Discussion

1. Write down your understanding of the Good News of God in Christ. What grounds this definition: Is it a biblical text? Something from our Church's tradition and liturgy? An experience that you've had?

2. The Baptismal Covenant in *The Book of Common Prayer* asks us to "proclaim by word and example the Good News of God in Christ" (p. 305). Who proclaims the Good News in these stories? Who receives the Good News? How do they respond?

3. Does each author in this section seem to understand the concept of Good News in a similar way or differently?

4. The Catechism in *The Book of Common Prayer* says that, "The mission of the Church is to restore all people to unity with God and each other in Christ" (p. 855). How do you define unity? What is it that binds us together? To be unified, do we all need to become the same?

5. In each of these stories, the Good News is proclaimed to different people, some of whom are Episcopalians and some of whom may not be. To whom do you think the Good News should be proclaimed? Should we limit our proclamation only to other Christians? Should we proclaim the Good News to those who are not Christians? If so, what do you think that looks like?

Prompts for Writing Your Spiritual Story

1. Recall a moment when someone proclaimed the Good News of God in Christ to you. How did you respond? How did you change because of this event?

2. Recall a moment when you proclaimed the Good News of Christ to someone else. What did proclamation feel like to you? Where was God in this event? How did you change as a result?

3. Recall a time when you participated in a mission activity. How was this event an example of proclaiming the Good News of God in Christ? How did you and/or the people you were working with change as a result? Did your relationship with God change as a result?

After you've selected a prompt, describe the event or moment and its significance to you in a story of a thousand words or less.

Closing Prayer

God, you proclaim the Good News through the story of Jesus Christ. In our own stories, help us to find and proclaim the Good News, that together with you, we may help create a world in which there is neither sorrow nor sighing but the joy of love eternal. Amen.

Visit **spiritualstories.forwardmovement.org** to read more stories—and, if you'd like, share your own.

Serving

Celebrant

Will you seek and serve Christ in all persons, loving your neighbor as yourself?

People

I will, with God's help.

DANIELLE ELIZABETH TUMMINIO

Singing God's Praise

I will open my mouth in a parable;
I will declare the mysteries of ancient times.

— PSALM 78:2,
THE BOOK OF COMMON PRAYER, P. 694

WHEN I WAS FIVE, my father brought home the soundtrack to the musical *Nunsense*, a comedy about nuns putting on a talent show to raise money to bury fourteen members of their order because the cook—Sister Julia, Child of God—accidentally poisoned them with her vichyssoise soup.

I did not know what vichyssoise soup was.

I did not know why the name Sister Julia, Child of God, was funny.

But I loved the music to *Nunsense*. I listened to it over and over again on audiocassette, mimicking the actresses' voices and their tap dancing feet, and in the midst of this absurd mélange of one nun doing a ventriloquist act and another yearning for the career she could have had as a ballerina, there was one serious track.

And I loved that track more than all the others.

"Growing Up Catholic" was performed by a character named Sister Robert Anne, who traded her rebellious Brooklyn childhood for the habit because the nuns at her Catholic school believed in her, wanted a better life for her than the one she was fashioning for herself.

There was yearning and melancholy in Sister Robert Anne's story, two feelings I wasn't old enough to have experienced. But they intrigued me. So I listened over and over again to this track about growing up and Vatican II, though I didn't know a shred about denominations—certainly not enough to understand that this one wasn't mine—and I earnestly believed Vatican II was a company that sold vats of cans.

So while a lot of the details went over my tiny head, what I did understand was that this actress had a beautiful voice. And because I wanted to sing just like her, I would imitate that voice—which was a curious combination of bell and belter—from the backseat of the car, my head tilted to one side, praying that I would inherit her voice one day, that I too would be a professional singer.

The actress sang:

> *At St. Clare's school, religion class*
> *begin with Mass each day.*
> *It was said in Latin then,*
> *that's how I learned to pray.*
> *The nuns appeared in black and white*
> *and so did every rule.*

The music got a little darker here, more intense.

> *But then the rules began to change*
> *and many lost their way.*
> *What was always black and white*
> *was turning shades of gray.*

I was so captivated by Sister Robert Anne's voice that I begged for months to see the musical. I told my parents I wanted to be a nun—because I thought they all tap danced and sang—and I wrote a letter to the actress, a woman named Christine, and said I would like to meet her.

Secretly, my father sent that letter to Christine and arranged for tickets, and one day after kindergarten, I came home to find a dress and hair bow and patent leather shoes laid out for me on my bed along with tickets to our evening adventure.

I don't remember much of the musical itself. What I do remember is that Christine had bronchitis, but she appeared that night because she didn't want to disappoint the little girl who wrote the letter. And I remember that when she met me after the show, she gave me the kind of hug you give someone you've known all your life, and then she took me out for cherry pie.

Cherry was my favorite kind of pie.

I only sporadically kept in touch with Christine over the years. Even though she wasn't a nun, she became my confidant, a confessor of sorts, and someone I looked up to as I grew as a person of faith and also as a professional singer.

I saw Christine for the last time a few years ago. She had been diagnosed with early onset Alzheimer's, and I met her at a café in Manhattan a few weeks before she moved into an assisted care facility. I didn't know if she'd remember me, if she'd remember that night when we shared my favorite kind of pie, I in patent leather Mary Jane's and she in character shoes.

Her sister brought her to the table, and I saw in her eyes a blankness that seemed to cover the aliveness that used to be there.

"I doubt she'll remember you," her sister said, as she helped her into the restaurant booth. "I'll go for a walk to give you some time."

Christine sat across from me in the booth, confused by the menu and looking at the fork as if she'd never seen one before. I moved to the other side of the booth to sit next to her, and suggested we order a decadent chocolate cake.

Chocolate cake was her favorite.

"Chocolate cake!" she exclaimed a few minutes later when the waitress delivered a slice enrobed in rich, swirly frosting. "Where did it come from?"

Too scared to ask if she remembered me, I sliced a chunk of the cake and handed her a forkful.

"I think you'll like it," I said.

She slid the fork into her mouth. "That may be the most delicious thing I've ever tasted," she said. Then she pointed the fork in my direction the way other people point a finger. "I remember you," she said. "You're the little girl who sings."

And then she sang, perfectly in tune, her voice lithe as a bird soaring toward the sun:

> *At St. Clare's school, religion class*
> *began with Mass each day...*

She placed the fork down and laid her hand on mine. "You gave me a gift today. You made me remember how to sing."

I wish I could say I seized that moment to tell Christine about how she gave me the gift of a lifetime of song. I wish I had told her that the yearning for music she instilled inside me led me to join an Episcopal Cathedral girls' choir—even though my parents preferred not to go to church—and that later I sang in a professional Anglo-Catholic choir. I wish I had told her how those experiences introduced me to God in such a profound way that I eventually left choral music for the priesthood.

But I didn't do any of those things. I sat stunned, holding the fork in midair until the chocolate cake on its tip fell to the plate. Christine's once hazy eyes pierced straight through me. She may not have remembered my name, but I had no doubt that she knew why our relationship mattered.

From Christine I discovered not only a love for music and a love for God, but also a deep wisdom: that what we take as given—what seems so black and white—will always turn a fuzzy gray. The timing may surprise; it may even alarm, and we will become different for it all. But while those experiences crack the foundation of our way of being in the world, gifts remain and relationships endure. Nothing changes that. Even when our life's song becomes a memory, and the memory begins to fade.

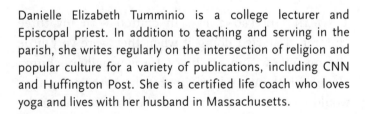

Danielle Elizabeth Tumminio is a college lecturer and Episcopal priest. In addition to teaching and serving in the parish, she writes regularly on the intersection of religion and popular culture for a variety of publications, including CNN and Huffington Post. She is a certified life coach who loves yoga and lives with her husband in Massachusetts.

BRUCE SMITH

A Front-Pew People

O Almighty God, who pourest out on all who desire it
the spirit of grace and of supplication:
Deliver us, when we draw near to thee,
from coldness of heart and wanderings of mind,
that with steadfast thoughts and kindled affections
we may worship thee in spirit and in truth;
through Jesus Christ our Lord.

— *THE BOOK OF COMMON PRAYER, P.* 833

I SIT IN THE FRONT PEW in church with my three children. I started doing it when they were very little and my wife was in seminary. I was usually in church alone with them, and I figured if they were noisy, they would be just as distracting in the back row as in the front, and they might be less fussy if they could see what was going on. There were only a few occasions when I had second thoughts, like the Easter morning when my son took his pants off during the sermon.

Before I moved up front, I had a half-held assumption that the closer a person sat to the altar, the more religious that person was. The truly devout, I thought, must kneel for the whole service in the front row, while those seeking after a spiritual truthiness (to paraphrase Stephen Colbert) cowered in the back row. But I never thought of myself as a religious person. My relationship with God has often been more a source of anxiety than a relief.

So although I wasn't sure I belonged there, I sat in the front row because it felt like a solution to a logistical problem: how to keep my young children—the children of a priest—engaged in church. After a year or so, I noticed other parishioners referring to the front pew as Bruce's row, and I once overheard the senior warden say to the treasurer, "You know Bruce—he sits in the front row." I puffed up with pride. I was not merely a clergy spouse. I was a front-pew person. It had become an identity, perhaps even with special powers like the Front Pew Piety Shield that could protect me from my own doubt, as well as from the militant atheists among my friends.

People started saving the pew for me. Even on busy Sundays if I was running late, the front pew would be there for me and my children. At the Feast of Saint Francis, we shared it with dogs, cats, snakes, and bunnies, but the front pew was still ours.

When my wife was called as rector at a new church, I thought, "But what about my pew?" In the midst of moving to a new state, leaving our network of family and friends behind, and looking for a new job of my own, I found myself wondering where I would sit in church.

She took up the reins of the new church, and I took my family right to the front pew. My youngest was still of an age where it helped to be able to see, and after all, it was his mother up there preaching, so he ought to get a good view. It was on one of those first Sunday mornings when I asked him if he was proud of his mother, who had the important title of rector. He patiently explained to me that, "Church is not exactly a kid's paradise."

Maybe not. And as my three children get bigger, the four of us no longer really fit in the front pew anymore. One day, sitting uncomfortably shoulder to shoulder and looking up at the simple cross above the altar, I realized that I was in the front row because, for me, it was closer to God. My God was in the front pew where there were fewer distractions, fewer heads bobbing back and forth, fewer lives with all their complications to consider as I meditated upon my particular anxiety-racked relationship with God. My half-formed and simplistic thought was correct: The closer I was to the representation of God, the closer I stood to salvation.

God is in the back pew too, of course, and all the pews in between. But I wasn't religious enough to find

God back there. I had to be up close for God's power to work in me. I realized that I wasn't sitting there so my children could see or to support my wife. I sat in the front pew because that's where God does his work on me, where God's strength and love gather me up in preparation for his work.

I know my children will settle into their own pew someday. It may be the front, or it may be the back. It may be in the choir stalls or in the narthex. The key to their relationship with God may not be in church at all. God will find them in their chosen pew at the time they most need to be found, and he will unlock their hearts. Then their human reasons and rationales for doing what they do will fall away, and, I hope, they will have a clear, unobstructed view of God's love like the one I have found sitting with them all the Sundays of their childhood in the front pew.

Bruce Smith is the chief development officer at Walnut Hill School for the Arts. He also writes plays, stories, and poems. His play *We Have Not Loved You With Our Whole Heart*, rooted in Episcopal themes, was produced in New York. He lives in Lincoln, Massachusetts, with his wife, the Rev. Kate Malin, and their three children.

KATHRYN BANAKIS

With Love,
the Road Not Taken

*Will you be responsible for
seeing that the child you present
is brought up in the Christian faith and life?*

— *THE BOOK OF COMMON PRAYER*, P. 302

LOOK, IT'S NOT LIKE A MESSENGER of the Lord appeared at my baptism and asked my parents, "For this girl baby, would you like her to live out her Christian commitment in the realm of family or career?" My parents didn't look new-parents-in-the-headlights at one another and whisper back: "career." Way too revisionist fairy tale.

Nor years later at my junior high confirmation, when I recommitted to my life as a baptized Christian,

When Two or Three Are Gathered

did an angel say, "When you daydream about adulthood, think about whether you want to attend to family or career first, because both don't usually emerge at the same time."

If that had happened, my parents and I both would have probably chosen for career to come first, which is what happened, but there just wasn't a cognizant choice at any one moment. And on the days when I start thinking I made some single wrong choice, my godsister Suzanne sets me right. Every baptized baby should get a godsister.

So here's what really happened: Suzanne and I met at a summer program for social justice and religion— two feisty, feminist teenage girls considering becoming pastors. It was like finding someone of our same exact type. At the end of the summer, we started writing old-fashioned letters back and forth. We wrote to stay awake through college lectures and through our first jobs, where we penned letters with equal passion about the injustices of labor policy and the annoyance of housemates eating the cereal we bought for ourselves.

In our mid-twenties, about the time I filled out applications for seminary, Suzanne filled out an application for a marriage license. And by the end of my seminary years, she had two sons. In the years since, we've settled into different roles, and the harried mom with a job who leads a small group at her church wonders about her career, while the priest wonders if her apartment will always be so quiet. We are both living out our Christian lives.

It's seductive to think that I would be happier or more sure or better rested if I'd made one critical decision differently. Maybe at some turning point in my life, I could have become Suzanne. But that's simply not true. Our letters back and forth tell the tale of life by a thousand small turns, all of which were prayerful and thoughtful and ultimately right because we lived into them. Neither of us was ever presented with the other person's situation and opportunities. And our letters make it clear that life would be no easier or happier as the other person, just different.

Godparents are important people to guide you along life's journey. But as an adult, my godsister has been even more so because she reminds me who I am and the reality of the choices I've made. Whenever I baptize a child, I wish for her a godsister, someone who will remind her of who she is as a child of God and guide her through the good, unique tangle of how she lives out her Christian life.

Kathyrn Banakis is an Episcopal priest who serves as community connector at St. Luke's Episcopal Church in Evanston, Illinois, and is a software trainer at a fundraising consulting firm for nonprofit organizations. She began her career as a federal lobbyist on issues of community development. Kat was a founding member of the Yale Divinity School chapter of The Beatitudes Society. Her introduction to progressive Christian theology for small groups, *Bubble Girl: An Irreverent Journey of Faith*, is available through Chalice Press.

Lamb of God

Send us now into the world in peace,
and grant us strength and courage
to love and serve you
with gladness and singleness of heart;
through Christ our Lord. Amen.

— *THE BOOK OF COMMON PRAYER, P.* 365

DURING A DIFFICULT TIME of transition in my life, God came to me in a dream. This vivid Technicolor dream broke through my sadness and brought me face-to-face with the love of God.

At the time I felt empty. All artists inevitably suffer a bout of creative block. Mine had been festering for several years, compounded by my family's moving to three different cities over a short period of time. The colors that had brought me such joy in years past seemed as faded, lonely, and tired as I felt after each move. I abandoned my canvases and worked only in my journals. My inspiration as an artist had escaped me, and the joy I found in painting—that gift of creation that always brought me closer to God—was gone.

But each Sunday in church I said aloud this part of the post-Communion prayer: "Grant us strength and courage to love and serve you." I prayed it into the deep place of ache that was my block. For strength to make it through these transitions and courage to be patient with myself. To once again love and serve God the best way I knew how, through my art and my life.

The post-Communion prayer, that plea for strength and courage and love, was layered into each page of the journals I kept during this time, along with my feelings of hurt and hope. And then I had the dream. I can still recall the details of that dream perfectly, though it's been more than a year.

I am on a yellow school bus, sitting beside my daughter as we drive through a verdant countryside. The bus stops for repairs, and I look out the window to see a flock of white sheep on the green hills in the distance.

With the fluidity of time and space that happens only in dreams, I am suddenly in the field with the sheep. They are close to me, and I can see the curls of coarse, cream-colored wool on their backs and the deep, black shine of their eyes. One sheep, much larger than the others, approaches me. I am filled with peace and calm. He pushes against me, the flat of his face against the hollow of my neck, like

an embrace that is strong and soft at the same time. I feel
an outpouring of love, real heart-bursting love, pushing and
pulsing into me.

In the moments after the dream, I found myself lying in my bed, suddenly wide awake. I put my hands to my neck and felt the pressure of that push, the warmth of the embrace.

"Jesus," I whispered to the darkness. I knew it as fully as I've ever known anything. Here was my Jesus, my Lamb of God.

Dreams are curious things, the work of the unconscious self that can seem sometimes more real than our waking reality. Author John Sanford calls dreams "God's forgotten language." Over and over in the Bible, characters receive revelations from God in dreams and visions. In both the Old and New Testaments of the Bible, we hear stories of such divine messages.

I have always had extraordinary dreams. I usually remember them in the morning and write down the ones that resonate. As an artist, I also feel a connection to the imagery in my dreams. Dream stories are nonlinear, jumping from one seemingly disconnected scene to another, incorporating people and events from disparate parts of my life. They rely on visual images and emotions, rather than words. Like dreams, my paintings are often visual stories, and as a mixed media artist, I collage images and colors from different sources to create a new dialogue of patterns and symbols.

The day after my dream, I kept reaching up to touch the place on my neck where the lamb had pushed against me. I was conscious of a heightened sense of awareness, almost a vibration in the air. I couldn't stop thinking about my sheep. This was a communion to feed my spirit and my creativity. I had to paint him.

I began layering words and paint on a large piece of heavy paper. I wrote my prayers into the layers, thanksgivings for this vision and this gift. One vibrant color followed another. Rich, saturated colors full of life and joy and promise. Bubblegum pink and sky blue, firecracker red and juicy orange—this was no white, fluffy sheep. This sheep was strong, pulsing with patterns of vivid pigments. This was my Technicolor Jesus. He filled me with peace and gladness, giving me strength and courage to paint again, pushing me into action. This Lamb of God was my Savior.

———■———

Caroline Coolidge Brown is a mixed media artist with an interest in both creating her own art and in teaching others to create. She spends her time working in her home studio and at the Wingmaker Arts Collaborative, where she teaches adult classes in mixed media painting and visual journaling. Currently based in Charlotte, North Carolina, she has held exhibitions throughout the United States.

HONDI DUNCAN BRASCO

The Peace of God

The peace of God, which passeth all understanding, keep your hearts and minds in the knowledge and love of God, and of his Son Jesus Christ our Lord; and the blessing of God Almighty, the Father, the Son, and the Holy Ghost, be amongst you, and remain with you always. Amen.

— *THE BOOK OF COMMON PRAYER*, P. 339

ON FRIDAY, MARCH 18, 1994, I was en route to the pediatrician's office on the Bronx River Parkway, frustrated by the slow traffic during a late snowstorm. Emily, our five-year-old, was holding a jar on her lap. Kate, our seven-year-old, was perplexed by the urgency of my voice. I had barely picked them up from school when the kindergarten teacher called to say that Emily had gone to the bathroom four times that morning.

When Two or Three Are Gathered

Who counts those things? But the fact registered in my brain, along with Emily's unusual eating habits for the past week. On Tuesday, after dinner, she had requested and consumed a bologna sandwich and washed it down with two glasses of water. Other than that, nothing was strange. She had no fevers, no symptoms. School and play dates had remained the same. I called our pediatrician, who was forty-five minutes away in New York City. He told me that Emily needed to be seen by the closest pediatrician.

"When?" I asked.

"Immediately. She needs a urinalysis," he said. I phoned a doctor in the next town who agreed to see us. The sample we brought confirmed the diagnosis, but just to be sure, the doctor ran a second test. Emily had Type I Diabetes, a disease that affects about one in four hundred children. Her pancreas had shut down and was producing little to no insulin, so the plan was to admit her to a hospital in New York City. My pediatrician in the city conferred with the local doctor and then spoke to me. "You don't need an ambulance, but get here as soon as possible."

I drove home, coordinated plans with my husband, Tom, and then called a friend who took Kate for the night. I was moving around our house on fast-forward, grabbing the things Emily and I might need. My husband called a car to take us from lower Westchester to New York City, so that in my current state of anxiety,

I would not be negotiating rush hour with a sick child in a storm.

I remember sitting in the backseat heading down the Deegan Expressway, across the Triborough Bridge and onto FDR Drive, holding Emily's hand. I recall the soft feel of her fingers, the string of red taillights, and the snow flakes. The last two hours had been a jumble of events and feelings. Twenty minutes into the drive to the city, I felt an inexplicable calm, a tranquility that defied the present circumstances, as if we were held by a different reality. I felt that God was sheltering and assuring us.

For reasons I will never understand, the peace that came over me the day our daughter was diagnosed did not leave me for the entire week she was in the hospital. It was there in the emergency room while my husband, daughter, and I waited with the overdosed, the victims of accidents, and the desperately ill. Together we shared our common helplessness as a kind of bond.

"Fear not," the voice of peace said, as Emily was having her blood drawn for the umpteenth time in a tiny examining room with a single table and sink.

"Peace I give to you," it whispered when she was finally admitted to a bed after midnight, hooked to an IV and clutching her yellow blanket.

"Not as the world gives," it murmured when Emily, awakened at 3:00 a.m. for a blood test, looked at me huddled under my jacket in the chair beside her and said, "Mom, it's so much fun spending the night with you."

In fact, that peace did not leave me for several weeks, as friends, family, and neighbors embraced our family in a vast network of care. Casseroles mysteriously appeared, and strangers who had children with diabetes became advocates and guides. Even now, I look back at that peace as pure gift, a grace to see us through. That year, difficult as it was, was also a moment of deep intimacy with God, a time that marked and changed me and claimed me in ways that I could not have imagined, sending me forward, confident of God's abiding love.

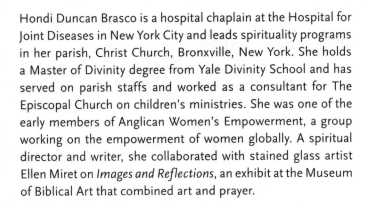

Hondi Duncan Brasco is a hospital chaplain at the Hospital for Joint Diseases in New York City and leads spirituality programs in her parish, Christ Church, Bronxville, New York. She holds a Master of Divinity degree from Yale Divinity School and has served on parish staffs and worked as a consultant for The Episcopal Church on children's ministries. She was one of the early members of Anglican Women's Empowerment, a group working on the empowerment of women globally. A spiritual director and writer, she collaborated with stained glass artist Ellen Miret on *Images and Reflections*, an exhibit at the Museum of Biblical Art that combined art and prayer.

Workshop Four

Opening Prayer

God, you call us to seek and serve Christ in all persons, and you call us to radical acts of neighborly love. Help us to seek and to serve you in everything that we do. Help us to love our neighbors richly and abundantly, and help us to love ourselves in the same way. As we grow in love for all that you have created, may our love for you grow in turn. Amen.

Questions for Discussion

1. Our Baptismal Covenant calls us to "seek and serve Christ in all persons" (*The Book of Common Prayer*, p. 305). What do you think it means to seek and serve Christ? Do you think it is possible to act this way with all people?

2. Who is seeking and serving Christ in each of these stories? How do they do it? Are there differences in the ways that they seek and serve that catch your attention?

3. Our Baptismal Covenant also calls us to love our neighbor as ourselves. Who is your neighbor? What do you think it means to love both neighbor and self the same way?

4. How do the people in the stories in this section exercise their understanding of love of neighbor and love of self?

5. Kat Banakis describes how loving her friend Suzanne at times made her question her own choices, even though the neighbor love she shares with Suzanne is incredibly transformative. How has loving your neighbor been a complicated act in your life? How has it made you grow?

Prompts for Writing Your Spiritual Story

1. Recall a moment where someone sought or served you in Christ. How did you respond? How did you change because of this event?

2. Recall a time when you sought or served another in Christ. How did that opportunity affect you and your relationship with God? How did it affect the other person or people?

3. Recall a moment when you loved your neighbor as yourself. How did you change as a result? Did your neighbors change? Where was God in this event?

After you've selected a prompt, describe the event or moment and its significance to you in a story of a thousand words or less.

Closing Prayer

God, in our acts of neighbor love, may we always be mindful to seek and serve you, because you do the same for us. Just as you sought the prodigal son, so you never stop seeking us out. Help us to see how our stories are shaped by the way that you continually seek and serve us, so that we might grow in wisdom and knowledge of you, until we become empowered to feel your love and to share it with all people. Amen.

Visit **spiritualstories.forwardmovement.org**
to read more stories—and, if you'd like, share your own.

Striving

Celebrant

*Will you strive for justice and peace
among all people, and respect the
dignity of every human being?*

People

I will, with God's help.

CAROLE MADDUX

Darkness Has Been Vanquished

He shall cover you with his pinions,
and you shall find refuge under his wings;
his faithfulness shall be a shield and buckler.
You shall not be afraid...

— PSALM 91:4,
THE BOOK OF COMMON PRAYER, P. 719

ONE SUMMER AT CHURCH CAMP when I was a teen, our spiritual exercise for the day was to draw a picture of when we were first aware of the presence of God. I drew the dawn.

That was the only way I knew to express that I had been blessed with the gift of a faith that seemed to have been with me all of my conscious life. Even as a very young child in Hawaii, I had an ever-present awareness

When Two or Three Are Gathered

that God was with me. Granted, at that point in my life my image of God was an odd amalgam of Santa Claus, Pele (the Hawaiian goddess of volcanoes), and Father DuTeil, the rector of St. Christopher's Episcopal Church in Kailua. No matter what God looked like, though, I knew God would never leave me, would always love me, and was, mysteriously, the source of me and all creation. I am so grateful God gave me the gift of faith. It became crucial to my life.

When my father, a career Marine, received orders to Vietnam in 1968, my family left the Pacific to live closer to our extended family on the east coast of the United States. This appeared to be a good idea because soon after my father left for the war, my younger brother and only sibling became critically ill and was hospitalized for long periods. With my father away and my mother tied up at the hospital with my brother, my primary caretaker after school and during the summer was my grandfather.

My grandfather was a milkman, so he came home earlier from work than my other relatives. He was also a pedophile. In 1968, no one taught children how to protect themselves, or even that adults might try to molest our bodies. We were all very vulnerable in a world that did not want to acknowledge that evil existed in our very own homes and that children could be victims.

So I had no idea how to tell an adult "no" or even whether the other adults in my life were complicit. My grandfather took advantage of that and sexually abused me from the age of eight until I was twelve. At that point, I announced to the family that I did not need a "babysitter" anymore and refused to be left alone with him any longer. There can be salvation hidden in a pre-teen's rebellion.

Despite, however, the blindness of the family, teachers, clergy, and church members around me to the abuse, my awareness of God's presence saved me. I knew, despite being raped by one who was supposed to care for me, that there was a God who really did care for me. Who was right there with me. Who valued me beyond my body or my obedience to adults. Who shared with me the pain and the isolation, yet kept a light shining in the darkness—a light I could cling to and follow throughout the abuse and the very difficult years that would follow.

The Book of Common Prayer was one of my touch-stones. On bad days, I would search through it for the words of the God I knew and to put into words some of the pain and confusion I felt. In many of those tough moments, the words of Psalm 91 would resonate with me:

> *He shall cover you with his pinions,*
> *and you shall find refuge under his wings;*
> *his faithfulness shall be a shield and buckler.*
> *You shall not be afraid...*

I was probably one of the only kids in my school who knew what pinions were!

Eventually, through the gifts and support of the rest of my family, talented therapists, supportive clergy, and the grace of God, I healed from the trauma of those years and went on to work with others isolated by pain, illness, or poverty. While I am with them to hear and understand *their* story and needs, my experience, I believe, grants a level of authenticity to my empathy. It gives me some street cred when I am working with the homeless and the mentally ill, and helps me to resist passing judgment when a child of God is acting out. I know that we often are completely unaware of the secrets of families and individuals.

Through that work, I began, too, to receive a call to the vocation of a deacon, called to "serve all people, particularly the poor, the weak, the sick, and the lonely." Ordained in 2006, I began the next year to serve at a street church for the homeless of Atlanta. Through that work, I feel and see anew the ever-present love of God in and for all his people. I continue to be healed and blessed by God as he allows me to serve those who struggle with mental illness, with addictions, with poverty and poor educations, with prison convictions and traumatic childhoods, and, yes, even those with sex offender status. People, just like me, who have found much needed comfort in Psalm 91.

As a deacon, I have the great privilege and prerogative to sing the ancient hymn of praise, the Exsultet, every year at the Easter Vigil. As I stand in the darkened church, illuminated only by the Paschal Candle, my faith and my gratitude for how it has sustained me fills and swells my voice as I sing:

> Rejoice and sing now, all the round earth,
>   bright with a glorious splendor,
>
> for darkness has been vanquished
> by our eternal King...

Holy Father, accept our evening sacrifice, the offering of this candle in your honor. May it shine continually to drive away all darkness. May Christ, the Morning Star who knows no setting, find it ever burning—he who gives his light to all creation, and who lives and reigns for ever and ever. Amen.

— THE BOOK OF COMMON PRAYER, PP. 286-287

Carole Maddux was ordained to the sacred order of deacons in 2006 in Atlanta. Her first assignment was to a suburban parish. Answering a call to serve the homeless and mentally ill, she was assigned to the Church of the Common Ground in January of 2007, where she still serves. Church of the Common Ground services are held in a city park. In 2008, she accepted an additional part-time assignment at an Anglo-Catholic parish. In 2011, she was appointed archdeacon of the Diocese of Georgia. In her diaconal ministry and day job, she directs Good Samaritan Health and Wellness Center, a free medical and dental clinic in Jasper, Georgia. She is blessed with two children and lives in Roswell with her husband and three rescue animals.

YEJIDE PETERS

A Cry Goes Up from My Soul

I know that my Redeemer liveth, and that he shall stand at the latter day upon the earth; and though this body be destroyed, yet shall I see God; whom I shall see for myself and mine eyes shall behold, and not as a stranger.

— *THE BOOK OF COMMON PRAYER, P. 469*

I DIDN'T KNOW I hadn't forgiven until the day I forgave. One day I woke up and the burden was lifted. I could not believe I had carried it fifteen years, through high school, college, my twenties, even through seminary.

I was fifteen the day I grew up. I remember my father getting a phone call, and there was a commotion down the hall. He came to my door and asked me to come to the living room. My father was—and is—a kind and gentle man. He rarely raises his voice, and I can count on one hand the times I've seen him cry. When my father spoke that day, I heard something in his voice I had never heard before and have never heard since: absolute desolation.

"I have some bad news. Shawn is dead."

If that was the day I grew up, surely it was the day my father became an old man. The day you tell your children their beloved cousin died in police custody is the day a part of your soul dies.

There is no way to catalog the suffering Shawn's death caused my family. Some things are too hard to imagine away. There is no movie or novel that can fully reach the depths of such a loss. A cry goes up from the soul—for the injustice! For the precious son lost! Who can know the suffering but the mother at the graveside, the father at the coffin, the brother who hoists the casket onto his youthful shoulder and bears the body from the church to the tomb?

There are few times that stay with me so vividly: the first time I fell in love, the first time I prayed and felt God, and the days and weeks after Shawn's death. I suppose it was also a first, for it was the first time I tasted the bitterness of death.

It was not within me to forgive the people who took my cousin's life. I was afraid that forgiving would diminish my love for Shawn, my passion for justice. I was afraid that forgiving would be something like accommodating the evil that allows a young black man to die and no one but his family and friends to mourn.

Yet every grief has a turning point, and mine was Ash Wednesday, 2006. My seminary was having a quiet day, and somewhere in the middle of the prayers and lectures it hit me. That year, I would be older than Shawn was on the day he died. He will forever be twenty-nine. He will never go gray. He will never hold a grandchild or forget where he has put his reading glasses. I was going where he had not. How could this be? Why should we live forever with mere photographs, with copies of his handsome smile and memories of his infectious laugh? Then I asked the question I had never dared: How could God have taken him?

And God began to move my heart.

I wanted Shawn back. I wanted to remember him completely. I did not want my only thought of him to be those terrible moments before he died. I wanted to hear the Sugar Hill Gang and not rush to turn off the radio because it hurt to listen to one of his songs. I wanted to remember him without the weight of my own anger and despair. I wanted to remember his smile, his laugh, the way he never met a stranger. Was there a dance he couldn't do or a joke he couldn't tell? He did everything with ease. He seemed to glide through life effortlessly, mastering each difficulty with a grace that eluded the rest of us. In the bright light of his joy, you couldn't help but feel at home. These are the things I longed to remember. This great and talented man deserved more than my tears. Shawn deserved to be remembered as he lived: in the bright light of the sun, not the shadows of death.

And God, who is so very good, gave that to me. It would be impossible to say exactly how, for who can fully comprehend the movement of grace? It was the comfort of others, the passage of time, the deepening of my own relationship with God. And finally, it was just grace—a pure gift, unearned and unexpected.

Years passed. I met many people who helped me heal, and I hope I did the same for them. When visiting South Africa, I encountered women and men who knew my story. They spoke of men strangled in jail cells and officially deemed suicides; they recounted the sorrowful tales of the disappeared. There was healing in knowing my family had not been singled out for some particular suffering. There is power in hearing another share a story so close to yours, it could be your own.

> *I know that my Redeemer liveth,*
> > *and that he shall stand at the latter day*
> > *upon the earth;*
>
> *and though this body be destroyed,*
> > *yet shall I see God;*
>
> *whom I shall see for myself*
> > *and mine eyes shall behold,*
>
> *and not as a stranger.*

God gave my soul a small resurrection. It is difficult to explain what forgiveness feels like—but if I had one word, I would say freedom. I am now free to remember Shawn and to laugh at the joy he brought to our lives. I am free to remember him anytime I choose, and the shadows of his final hours cannot take away my joy. For I know that my Redeemer liveth. We will see God. *We* will see God, though our bodies be destroyed—yet shall we see God. And Shawn already sees.

As long as I hated those involved in the final hours of my cousin's life, I was not free. The shadows of their deeds crowded out all the complexity of his life. Now, when the sadness and anger come, I pray for those who were complicit in my cousin's death. I cannot forget them. I grieve daily for the empty space in the lives of my dear aunt and uncle. I pray and work for the day of justice, for the day when no mother or father has to hear those terrible words, "Your son is gone." I know God is bringing this to pass, maybe not in my time, but in God's time. And so I ask, thy kingdom come.

I know that my Redeemer liveth. No matter what we feel like on this side of heaven, death and evil are not the final word. The final word is Love.

Yejide Peters is an Episcopal priest and (often disappointed) New York Mets fan. She currently serves as rector of All Saints' Episcopal Church in Briarcliff Manor, New York. She is passionate about peace-building, theology, writing, music, silly jokes, cooking, and spending time with friends and family.

Journey of Faith

Heavenly Father, send your Holy Spirit into our hearts, to direct and rule us according to your will, to comfort us in all our afflictions, to defend us from all error, and to lead us into all truth; through Jesus Christ our Lord. Amen.

— THE BOOK OF COMMON PRAYER, P. 107

I WAS BROUGHT UP AS A ROMAN CATHOLIC, and I took my faith seriously, even though I was forced to be an altar boy and to memorize Latin prayers I didn't understand. I lived in mortal terror of ever doing something wrong. I had a non-church-going violent alcoholic father who attacked me physically twice. My mother had a morbid fear of churches. I was sent to "Cat-lick" school for nine years in which the priests, nuns, and brothers routinely maintained order by being verbally and physically abusive to their students. This went on until I was expelled from a Catholic high school. At the age of fifteen, I was sent to a public high school but was still forced by my parents to go to church.

In my late teens, I grew more and more dissatisfied with many aspects of Catholicism and the church I attended. For one thing, there was a priest who would shout verbally abusive remarks at young people while in the confessional so they would be humiliated when they reappeared from behind the curtain. For another, I encountered priests and nuns who were anti-Semitic, which bothered me because I had a lot of Jewish teachers and friends and found them to be very good and welcoming people. Finally, there was The Index and The Legion of Decency. The Index was a list of forbidden books, and The Legion of Decency kept a list of forbidden movies that, once a year, during Mass, you swore an oath to not see. This presented a problem for me. In addition to preventing intelligent inquiry, the ban included many books that were required reading in college, among them, the works of authors like Voltaire, Sartre, Hugo, Flaubert, Balzac, Machiavelli, and even Galileo—because officially the world was still flat according to the Roman Catholic Church.

When I started college at New York University, I heard this line that really resonated with me: "You are never a great writer until the Catholic Church condemns your work."

Then came the breaking point. I went to church one Sunday, and I heard a sermon in which the priest (under orders from the New York City cardinal) endorsed, from the pulpit, a political stance about the war in Vietnam with which I disagreed. Then he told us that as good Catholics, we had to share the same opinion as the Church did. I felt this insulted my ability to think individually and to draw my own conclusions based on my own faith experiences.

As a result of these years of built-up anger with the Catholic Church and after hearing that sermon, I got up from my seat and walked up the main aisle through the doors and into the fresh air. From that day almost until I got married, on Sunday mornings when I was supposed to be in church, I went to the local soda fountain shop.

However, sometime in the 1970s while in England with my wife, I attended an Evensong in Lincoln Cathedral. As I sat there, for the first time in a very long time I did not feel like a tourist seeing the great churches of Europe. I was perfectly comfortable and at peace. This single event proved to be a life-changing experience. After that, I did some investigation about Anglicanism and The Episcopal Church, and I began to wonder if this could be my home.

My wife became pregnant in 1980. When our daughter started asking incessant questions about God, I remembered my experience in Lincoln Cathedral and what I had learned subsequently about The Episcopal

Church. So even though I'd stayed away from church for over a decade, I thought I might give this new denomination a chance. After I attended some services at The Cathedral of The Incarnation on Long Island, a young priest, Father Rick McCall, came to our house to talk with me. I peppered him with questions, especially about how the Church would care for my daughter, as I did not want her to have the same experiences with faith that I had as a child.

"I am lending you my daughter and not giving her to you. Please do right by her, or I will take her away from you," I told him. He listened and affirmed my sentiment, and I thought that this could be a place that my family and I could call our spiritual home. I knew for sure when Father McCall told me he remembered that conversation several years later. He said, "I went to your house with the intention of interviewing you. Instead, you interviewed me."

I'd never had that kind of experience with organized religion before.

Little by little, my whole family became active in the cathedral. My daughter spent a decade of her childhood singing her heart out in the girls' choir. My wife became active in the Service League, and I was a lay eucharistic minister for eleven years.

When I think about that journey into The Episcopal Church, I see how my childhood experiences in the Roman Catholic Church led me to Lincoln Cathedral, and I see how that moment in Lincoln led me to become an Episcopalian. Even though life may be a series of vignettes that we can't interpret with certainty until the very end, there are some things we can learn along the way, and some moments that change the course of our journey forever.

———■———

Gregory Tumminio is a New York University graduate and a former educator. He was also a lay eucharistic minister and thurifer. At one time or another, he has also been a writer, journalist, dramaturg, actor, painter, and photographer. He has ongoing interest in religion, classical music, theater, art, and cooking. He has been married for forty-four years, has one daughter, and was recently diagnosed with a rare nerve disorder, primary lateral sclerosis.

WHITNEY Z. EDWARDS

The Hard Wood of the Cross:

A Short Reflection on Salvation

Lord Jesus Christ,
you stretched out your arms of love
on the hard wood of the cross
that everyone might come within the reach
of your saving embrace...

— *THE BOOK OF COMMON PRAYER*, P. 101

I WENT TO PRISON looking for my brother. Not so much for him as for what had *happened* to him, and to us. Though the crime was his alone, we had all suffered: me, our sister, mom, and dad. His alcohol-drenched car accident, the deaths of others, the news articles, the shame and deafening silence of friends—we had borne it all and it broke us. Not long after my brother's incarceration, our father drank until he died, and our mother did the same, only a little more slowly. I was left to my own devices at such a young age that I shudder to think what could have happened after leaving home with few possessions and a load of pain.

But what did happen, instead, was grace, in the form of a grandmother who needed me almost as much as I needed her. Her home became mine when I was fifteen, and it stayed that way until she died ten years later. It is because of those years with her that I can confidently say I was saved in the embrace of her honest living, her steady and reliable love, and in the hold of the church pew that she, her father, and her father's father had worn well with use. Her simple brick home on a slow-moving river was a refuge from which I could venture out and begin to make sense of a world that seemed dangerously fickle and beset with unreasonable cruelty.

I was never allowed to visit my brother in a prison deep in the south. But a short ways down the river that ran beneath my bedroom window, there was a jail. So, I began my search there, which, as best I could tell, was the closest I could get to him and the events that had laid waste to our family and my innocence. The jail was made of block and steel and armed with friendly guards whose sisters I knew. The first time I went inside was as a chapel helper, and I hid behind a large volunteer named Peggy who loved the inmates fiercely and foolishly, and talked about Jesus as if she knew him.

Peggy acted as if those addicts and indigents were saints in wolfskins, while I was politely terrified of them all and stood next to the door and within sight of nearby guards (never have I been more glad to see a shotgun). My eyes studied floor tiles for the entire hour, and I breathed better as the last pair of cheap prison-issued shoes shuffled out. As Peggy gathered her things, she turned to me saying, "Well, that went well. Come back next week?" I didn't say no.

Week after week, I returned to the jail, carrying only questions at first and later photocopies and Bibles, changing my work schedule to nights so I could go to the jail during the day. I started nodding at first and then speaking at times, and within months I was leading services according to *The Book of Common Prayer*, which I had hardly known but for its resting place in the pews at my grandmother's church.

The men seemed to respect me, and my words seemed somehow important in there, while outside they always got lost in the chaos of the unincarcerated. Worn out by the constant din of hard words and even harder people, the men liked praying the psalms in slow, hushed tones, allowing the ancients to do the feeling for them. I'd tell them they were safe there, safe enough even to close their eyes, and they would, with relief, and tears would pour out over dull, tattooed skin.

I'd welcome new guys who were bug-eyed with terror and nod farewell to the lifers on their way to long-term facilities set in the soy fields along where the river grew even wider. They'd share stories of childhoods loaded with pain, and adulthoods traded for regret, and lovers lost but never forgotten. I'd bring their families to them on Saturdays, because jails are never on the bus line. Babies would whine with the itch of collars whiter than the heavenly host, and girlfriends would nervously smooth their tight jeans, anticipating the touch of their man. My car would smell like a beauty parlor for days after. I watched from the corner of the visiting room as conversations about report cards and broken car parts and sick relatives and tight budgets were shared over long metal tables, with every word carefully heard to be remembered for days and weeks after. The time moved impossibly fast, and nerves would quicken as guards cleared their throats, anxious to get the men locked back up.

Eventually, I came to know prison wardens and judges, legislators, and bishops, and I was hired on to oversee the ministries of every jail, juvenile facility, and prison in the state of Virginia. I was ordained a priest in The Episcopal Church because I came to find words wanting and the sacraments inexplicably powerful. But, of course, I didn't go to jail looking for my life's purpose: I went to find fellowship with the broken, the burdened, and the blamed. I sought kinship in those who had suffered evils not spoken of in polite company, and among them I came to know beauty beyond all evidence to the contrary and forgiveness for that which I cannot understand. And, most unexpectedly, in between the bars and gates and rolls of razored wire, I kept meeting this character Jesus, who, it seems, had long awaited me. Jesus, who stretched out his arms upon the hard wood of the cross so that everyone might come within the reach of his saving embrace, was there living among men who had known and caused suffering beyond measure.

I found Jesus wrapped in ill-fitting button-downs and bad tattoos. I found him in old white men choking on bitterness and young black men whose potential had drowned in meaningless monotony. I glimpsed him in the addict whose incarceration had saved his life and in the poor whose names were forgotten by court-appointed attorneys. Jesus was in the guard who slipped magazines to the guys in solitary and in the librarian who fought to get a GED in men's hands before they were let loose in a world waiting to eat them up.

I went to prison looking for what had broken in me, and by the grace of God I found Jesus and returned home every evening to tell my grandmother about him. And somewhere, on that short stretch of river between the two, I was saved.

Whitney Z. Edwards is an Episcopal priest serving a parish in Portland, Oregon, with her husband, Chris, and their daughter, who is named Emmeline Frances, after her grandmother. Whitney still loves prison ministry and insists upon always living within a stone's throw of a slow-moving river.

Workshop Five

Opening Prayer

God, you call us to strive for justice and peace among all people. You call us to respect the dignity of everyone. Help us to notice those in need, even when others in our society overlook them. Help us to right wrongs, even when it makes us unpopular. Help us to create peace, even when peace seems impossible. As we embark upon all of these things, be present with us, motivate, guide, and support us, so that together we may inaugurate your kingdom. Amen.

Questions for Discussion

1. Our Baptismal Covenant asks us to "strive for justice and peace among all people" (*The Book of Common Prayer*, p. 305). What does the word justice mean to you? What tools does our Episcopal tradition give us to bring it about?

2. What does the word peace mean to you? What tools does our tradition give us to bring it about?

3. The Baptismal Covenant does not ask that we accomplish justice and peace, but rather that we *strive* for it. Why do you think this particular word was chosen? Do you think it is possible for us to accomplish justice and peace, with God's help? How do the authors of the stories in this section either strive for or accomplish justice and peace?

4. Our Baptismal Covenant asks us to "respect the dignity of every human being" (*The Book of Common Prayer*, p. 305). What does that phrase mean to you? How do you think respecting a person's dignity is the same or different from loving one's neighbor?

5. How do the writers of this section respect the dignity of a person or persons? What do you think motivates them to do so?

Prompts for Writing Your Spiritual Story

1. Recall a moment when you experienced an injustice. Did someone respect your dignity during this time? What changed in you and your faith life as a result?

2. Recall a moment when you did not respect the dignity of another human being. Where was God in this event? Why did it leave a lasting impression on you?

3. Recall a time when you sought for justice or peace on someone else's behalf. How did that opportunity affect you, your relationship with God, and the other person?

After you've selected a prompt, describe the event or moment and its significance to you in a story of a thousand words or less.

Closing Prayer

God, by telling our stories, we begin to realize the ways that you call us to acts of justice, peace, and respect. May we continue to tell our stories and to hear the stories of others, so that we may grow in our ability to accomplish these ideals on your behalf. Make us strong in faith and always willing to share your presence in our lives, so that others may feel empowered to tell their stories as well. By sharing these narratives, may we know ourselves and our neighbor better, and become more closely linked to you as well. Amen.

Visit **spiritualstories.forwardmovement.org**
to read more stories—and, if you'd like, share your own.